# SHAMAN ISIS

# MEMORY MANSION
## HOW TO GLOW THE FU%K UP

Copyright ©2023 by Shaman Isis

All rights reserved.

No portion of this book may be reproduced in any form without written permission from the publisher or author, except as permitted by U.S. copyright law.

Dedication: For my son Garrett, I love you very much. P.S. I better not catch you dropping f-bombs after this!

For my mother Doris, father Dean, and sister Deanna, who left this world far too young, we did it; we broke the chain of pain.

For everyone who gifted me with life lessons that made me a wiser woman, thank you from the bottom of my healed heart.

# Contents

| | | |
|---|---|---|
| | Special Note: | XIII |
| 1. | Chapter 1<br>Age 23, San Diego | 1 |
| 2. | Chapter 2<br>Age 23, San Diego | 3 |
| 3. | Chapter 3<br>Age 23, San Diego | 5 |
| 4. | Chapter 4<br>Age 18, Collierville | 8 |
| 5. | Chapter 5<br>Age 18, Mom's | 10 |

6. Chapter 6                                        12
   Age 5, The Orphanage

7. Chapter 7                                        15
   Age 8, The Orphanage

8. Chapter 8                                        17
   Age 8, The Orphanage

9. Chapter 9                                        20
   Age 8, The Orphanage

10. Chapter 10                                      23
    Age 38, NYC

11. Chapter 11                                      25
    Age 9, The Orphanage

12. Chapter 12                                      27
    Age 9, The Orphanage

13. Chapter 13                                      30
    Age 9, The Orphanage

14. Chapter 14                                      32
    Age 9, The Orphanage

15. Chapter 15                                      35
    Age 12, Mom's

| | | |
|---|---|---|
| 16. | Chapter 16<br>Age 29, NYC | 40 |
| 17. | Chapter 17<br>Age 29, NYC | 42 |
| 18. | Chapter 18<br>Age 26, NYC | 45 |
| 19. | Chapter 19<br>Age 7, Memphis | 50 |
| 20. | Chapter 20<br>Age 12, Memphis | 52 |
| 21. | Chapter 21<br>Age 12, Mom's | 55 |
| 22. | Chapter 22<br>Age 13, Memphis | 61 |
| 23. | Chapter 23<br>Age 14, Collierville | 65 |
| 24. | Chapter 24<br>Age 30, NYC | 70 |
| 25. | Chapter 25<br>Age 30, NYC | 74 |

| | | |
|---|---|---|
| 26. | Chapter 26<br>Age 14, Collierville | 78 |
| 27. | Chapter 27<br>Age 50, 2020 | 82 |
| 28. | Chapter 28<br>Age 23, San Diego | 84 |
| 29. | Chapter 29<br>Age 25, New York | 90 |
| 30. | Chapter 30<br>Age 13, Mom's | 93 |
| 31. | Chapter 31<br>Age 13, Mom's | 97 |
| 32. | Chapter 32<br>Age 13, Collierville | 101 |
| 33. | Chapter 33<br>Age 14, Collierville | 106 |
| 34. | Chapter 34<br>Age 26, NYC | 110 |
| 35. | Chapter 35<br>Age 26, NYC | 114 |

| | | |
|---|---|---|
| 36. | Chapter 36<br>Age 26, NYC | 117 |
| 37. | Chapter 37<br>Age 6, The Orphanage | 121 |
| 38. | Chapter 38<br>Age 9, The Orphanage | 124 |
| 39. | Chapter 39<br>Age 13, Mom's | 129 |
| 40. | Chapter 40<br>Age 8, The Orphanage | 133 |
| 41. | Chapter 41<br>Age 32, NYC | 137 |
| 42. | Chapter 42<br>Age 30, NYC | 140 |
| 43. | Chapter 43<br>Age 12, Mom's | 145 |
| 44. | Chapter 44<br>Age 13, Mom's | 149 |
| 45. | Chapter 45<br>Age 29, NYC | 153 |

46. Chapter 46     157
    Age 31, NYC

47. Chapter 47     160
    Age 12, Mom's

48. Chapter 48     163
    Age 12, Mom's

49. Chapter 49     166
    Age 12, Mom's

50. Chapter 50     172
    Age 32, NYC

51. Chapter 51     176
    Age 36, NYC

52. Chapter 52     180
    Age 8, The Orphanage

53. Chapter 53     183
    Age 13, Mom's

54. Chapter 54     187
    Age 38, NYC

55. Chapter 55     193
    Age 17, Collierville

| | | |
|---|---|---|
| 56. | Chapter 56<br>Age 16, Collierville | 197 |
| 57. | Chapter 57<br>Age 36, NYC | 200 |
| 58. | Chapter 58<br>Age 38, NYC | 206 |
| 59. | Chapter 59<br>Age 40, NY | 214 |
| 60. | Chapter 60<br>Age 12, Mom's | 219 |
| 61. | Chapter 61<br>Age 50, South Florida | 223 |
| 62. | Chapter 62<br>Age 40, New York | 228 |
| 63. | Chapter 63<br>Age 51, South Florida | 235 |
| 64. | Chapter 64<br>Age 51, South Florida | 238 |
| 65. | Chapter 65<br>Age 51, South Florida | 243 |

66. Chapter 66 247
    Age 52, South Florida
67. Chapter 67 252
    Age 53, NYC

## Special Note:

This book is a memoir. It reflects the author's recollections of experiences over time. Some names have been changed, some events have been compressed, and some dialogue has been recreated. For clarity, ages and years are close approximations.

# Chapter 1

## AGE 23, SAN DIEGO

The light on my answering machine was blinking. I rarely receive messages at home. I walked over and hit play.

"Hey, Cindy. Hopefully, you recognize my voice. I wanted to warn you that people are looking for you again. I am sure it's because every hair salon around Tennessee has a poster of your face. I was surprised the first time I saw it. Paul Mitchell, wow. I am glad you are doing well, but I think the poster has given your location away. You asked me to call if anything like this happened. Now may be a good time to get lost," the message said.

"Shit," I dropped to the couch.

SHAMAN ISIS

Weird things have been happening lately. People were following me.

I almost always knew. It came from a lifetime of practice—one of the many reasons I didn't let anyone get too close to me. Deep down, I felt stained by my history.

I should have asked more questions about the modeling job I had booked. At 5'7 with brown hair and brown eyes, I was fortunate to secure the gig. Exotic wasn't popular at the time.

It turned out to be a national ad campaign. The company had shipped my poster to almost every damn salon in the country.

God, I was finally starting to like San Diego.

It was time to run again.

I would have to get more creative in the next city.

I could try Los Angeles, but I was not a fan. People are obsessed with what you do for a living. I preferred to avoid people asking me questions designed to determine my usefulness.

# Chapter 2

## AGE 23, SAN DIEGO

"Oh, shit. Shit, shit, shit," I mumbled.

I could not believe my eyes. It was Jimmy, the man who had made my childhood so weird.

God, I felt like I was going to throw up. I turned and started speed walking in the opposite direction. My heart was banging in my ears. I couldn't breathe.

I pulled my knife out and slid the blade between my fingers. One too many kidnapping attempts had made me hyper-vigilant. I had been carrying a knife since I was young.

Wow, Jimmy was here. That man! I should have expected this. I was hoping that I was just being jumpy. Nope, they had found me, and now he was here.

My foster father was strictly blue-collar. I would never believe he could hire the men who had followed me.

The men who stalked me drove nice cars and carried cameras and binoculars. Sometimes, they had notepads and, on occasion, wore a uniform.

Jimmy threw the details of what I did in my face. Details he could only know if my spies were informing him. That is how I knew there was a connection between the two situations. They were telling him what they were observing. That was clear.

At one time, I had seen him as a father figure. That was back during my days at Saint Peter's Orphanage. He ruined that illusion right after I became a ward of the state again. This time, he and his wife took over my custody.

I worked hard to get away from them. They showed up in the city I escaped to over a year ago.

I was concerned. Maybe Jimmy and his friends were worried I would tell someone about what happened growing up in Memphis.

My childhood had been less than ideal. Standards of the day labeled it unfortunate.

I was going to have to be more innovative in the next city.

First, I was going to get some help starting over.

# Chapter 3

## Age 23, San Diego

I could not believe Jeff appeared in a genuine FBI spy van. Ha, if he only knew why I wanted to talk to him.

I told him I needed advice on getting away from someone terrible. He assumed I meant my first weak attempt to disguise my identity.

I had already told my soon-to-be ex I had made a colossal mistake. I married my first husband to get a new name and hide while I figured out how to get out of Tennessee.

No joke. We got married right after meeting each other. The judge took a short break from a murder trial to do the deed. Romantic, it was not.

The whole scene said everything about the state of my life. What can I say? I was desperate.

## SHAMAN ISIS

My soon-to-be-ex followed me when I ran to California and soon accepted that we were not suitable for each other.

Anyway, he was not the reason I had contacted the FBI.

I probably should have told Jeff the truth, but I had never figured out how powerful the men who had watched me were. My intuition and the fact that it took money and organization to follow a young girl for years made me suspect things that could ruin lives and reputations.

I calmed my visceral reaction to the vehicle. Growing up, I had many close encounters with men in strange vehicles, escaping more than one in my day.

He slid the door open, and I was surprised to see that it was a stripped-down version of a movie spy van. There were two seats in front and panels of equipment on the sides. He sat on a chair next to the listening equipment.

I was suitably surprised. Well, I needed help. So, I did not feel bad that Jeff had met me at a gas station in the middle of the day. Jeff was tall with short brown hair and had the build of a former college football player. He handled his size with grace.

I climbed in and sat in the chair opposite him. I was immediately comfortable because he always behaved like a gentleman. I had rented him and another FBI agent an apartment. That is how we met.

He asked me to explain what I needed. I told him I needed to disappear. I kept my story as close to the one he had assumed. I was sure he knew when people were lying. I did not want to lie to an acquaintance, especially someone willing to help me.

Lying by omission was something I was very practiced at doing. It always made me feel guilty to frame my experience in a way that made my origins a mystery.

Jeff explained that his best friend's fiance had dealt with an abusive stalker, and he had seen firsthand how difficult it was to get help. His sincerity was touching.

We talked for a while about ways I could hide in plain sight. I clarified that I wanted to be successful while protecting my real identity. Jeff gave me tips on how to make it harder to be found.

Little did I know that it would be 30 years before I would use my real name. In retrospect, I was simultaneously terrified and fearless.

# Chapter 4

## AGE 18, COLLIERVILLE

I woke up with a start. It was the third time I had that vision this week. I know what that means from years of experience. It wasn't a dream. It was a disturbing memory from when I was a baby.

It started the same each time. I was lying on my back in my crib in Germany. I came awake knowing that my mom needed help. She was distressed.

I stood in my crib and began navigating the 70's era railing designed to keep me safe. I slid over the top and dropped to the ground. Walking on my own was still new for me.

The house was dark and quiet. My small size distorted the hallway.

I remember feeling very focused on finishing what I had started, finding my mom. I used the wall and faint light to make my way.

When I finally reached the bathroom door, I knew what I would see but pushed it open.

The sight that greeted me was even more brutal than in my dream. My mom was falling off the toilet onto the bathroom floor. There was a bloody mess everywhere.

I fully registered the disturbing scene. My mom was too far gone to speak.

I opened my mouth and let out cries so loud they brought help.

# Chapter 5

## AGE 18, MOM'S

The next time I saw my mom, I brought the dream up. We were trying to repair a relationship damaged by her putting me in care as a child. We never argued, but her boomer-era silence confused me about our family history.

She was washing dishes, something she did to relax. My mom was a beautiful woman, not conventionally pretty because of her prominent nose, but she was voluptuous, had legs for days, and had stunning blue eyes.

I asked her about the memory. I saw her knees give, and the plate she was soaping fell to the floor with a shatter.

When she recovered her breath, she turned to me and said, "Cindy, they said there was no way you would ever be able to remember that. You were a baby."

Although I knew it was a memory, I was still shocked. Mom never mentioned having a miscarriage. She explained that the doctor advised her never to bring it up. Due to my father's absence and him being the only other person who knew, that was easy to accomplish. The doctor also told her that memories were impossible in young children.

It is a hell of a first-life memory. I added it to the rooms inside my head.

As a child, I decided to store every memory I wanted to keep. So, I designed a mansion of rooms in my mind that held my good and bad experiences. I put the memories in boxes and tucked them on shelves mounted on the walls in each room, labeled by importance.

I call it memory mansion. Those memory rooms helped me make sense of things I would not speak about for decades.

# Chapter 6

## AGE 5, THE ORPHANAGE

I was (again!) on my back, looking at the ceiling. Only this time, I was performing to make the other children laugh. Most days, I could feel pain rolling off of the other kids. It was far greater pain than any tears would show.

I didn't cry the day my mom dropped me at Saint Peter's Home for Children, which, thank God, was no longer called Saint Peter's Asylum. I was already used to being an adult in a child's body.

I remember clocking in that the orphanage was safe, warm, and run by nuns. It was also a massive, old, rambling estate that reminded me of the fairy tales I loved. It seemed like a much better option than living in a car, a terrible experience for a young mom and three small children.

When new kids arrive, the older kids give them comfort. I remember discussing what we should and shouldn't say to the newbies. They appreciated the hugs and pep talks.

When someone was troubled, I would try to make them laugh. That is what got me my first ass-whooping from Sister Mary Rose. She was an angry, plain-faced woman who wore her habit as armor.

I was pretending to give birth to a baby doll. I hid the doll under my dress and then put on a show of pushing her out. The children were laughing at my antics when the room became quiet. I knew I was in trouble.

The sisters preferred order.

I could feel one of them standing over my head. She had her hands on what I thought were her hips. It's hard to say with those baggy habits. When I opened my eyes, I saw the complete shock on her face. She was confused about how I even knew about babies.

I would figure that out years later when I had a recurring dream.

When she caught the smirk on my face, she dragged me ear first to the paddle post. The next thing I knew, I was given wacks with a giant wooden plank.

Most of the nuns were kind, like the saintly Sister Anne Elizabeth. Only a few qualified as evil in my book. Sister

Mary Rose was one of them. All the kids were afraid of her.

I swear she enjoyed the beatings. She struck hard and didn't care about aiming. She always seemed relieved afterward.

Of course, it was her, the mean nun. That is how I have always thought of her.

I took great joy in provoking her when I was feeling rebellious.

## Chapter 7

# AGE 8, THE ORPHANAGE

I was running through the streets of Memphis on my own again. Checking on the people I had come to know whenever I snuck out of Saint Peter's. I was comfortable in the city.

In the 70s, Memphis music was everywhere. Nearly everyone I befriended had some instrument, even if it was a harmonica. I would hang out with anyone who was playing.

I got to know some wonderful people.

My secret escapades were the highlight of my time at Saint Peter's. I would sneak out when the Sisters were busy. That was easy since they did a lot of praying, cooking, and cleaning.

That left plenty of time for me to explore. I would squeeze through the gates and go on adventures.

Minding rules was never my strong suit. Breaking them would become something of a signature in my glamorous future career.

I had already been speaking to my spirit guides, made up of my angels, ancestors, and higher self, for years. They were my companions and whispered advice at crucial moments.

They told me to seek my education in the streets. They chorused that it was preparation for my future. So, that is where I spent my free time.

My guides hinted that I thought differently and would learn more independently. I don't think they understood how to explain autism in the early 70s.

I was saying hi to Ray-Ray when I realized I needed to return. Ray-Ray was skinnier than me and slightly taller. He had leathery dark skin and wise eyes. He always perked up when he saw me.

I might lose my precious freedom if I don't return in time. Running and freedom are something of a theme in my life.

## Chapter 8

## AGE 8, THE ORPHANAGE

I was sitting in a giant box of stuffed animals. The photographer told me to smile big, and perhaps someone would adopt me. He assumed I wanted to be adopted. I did not. I wanted to live with my mother.

It was summertime. That meant the orphanage's biggest fundraiser was coming up. I wouldn't say I liked being a model for fundraising ads, but it allowed me to enjoy some exciting moments.

Once, they took me to the front gates for a photo shoot with the unofficial mayor of Memphis, Elvis.

It's not nearly as unbelievable as it sounds. The truth is Graceland was around the corner, and Elvis supported the work of Saint Peter's. I was there at the right time.

I didn't understand why everyone was acting so weird. I did know that Elvis was important. My memory of him is vivid.

I will have a much more exciting encounter with him soon enough.

That was one photo of the orphan model my mother wished she had. She heard about the shoot from the Sisters.

One day, she opened the *Memphis Press-Scimitar* to find a giant photo of me that said, adopt this smiling face. That is how she found out about modeling.

I remember that photo shoot as they put me smack between two boys. I was on my stomach with my chin resting on my hand and a smile on my face.

She was upset that they used me as a "model" without her permission to raise funds for an orphanage she regretted putting us in. I understood why it bothered her and tried not to bring it up.

She felt they were turning me into a target for perverts. I only wished I could tell her how right she was to be concerned.

She kept those newspaper clippings secret for a long time. I would find them among her papers over the years. She used everything from a clear Tupperware bread box to a black cigar box as a safe.

She told me she kept them in case she needed to speak about what "really happened" back then. She would hint that they owed our family. She meant the absurd institutions of the 70s. I never felt she resented the Sisters or the vital work they did.

# Chapter 9

## AGE 8, THE ORPHANAGE

God knows where my father was when we were in Saint Peter's. He fell apart after a horrific accident on the autobahn in Germany.

I was born in Frankfurt in 69. My father was in the Army and stationed there.

We flew to the States with my dad in a hospital bed. Back then, they didn't understand what long periods of pain medication did to people prone to addiction.

My few memories of my father are not the stuff of dreams. He was exotic and charming and thought of me as his mini-me. He made a great Donald Duck impression. However, I could always tell that he was high.

As a baby, I remember trying to wake him in the mornings, and his eyes would roll back in his head.

I would bounce on his stomach to try to rouse him. If that didn't work, I would scrounge food from the kitchen, usually candy or whatever didn't require cooking.

Once, my mother came home to find me on top of the kitchen cabinets, trying to get a food bag. My dad was out cold. She was pissed because I was far too young to be feeding myself.

Soon, he would be gone, and we would be homeless.

That finally brought my mother to the door of Saint Peter's.

I remember how upset she was the day they took us in. She didn't have to cry for me to feel her sorrow.

Somehow, she was the strongest and most fragile woman I have ever known—well-used muscle over a glass skeleton.

I have always resented the inference that she was morally weak. Somehow, of lesser stock. I always wondered if she was inadequate in ensuring we were safe; what did that make wealthy parents who shipped their kids off to private school?

My mother's silence and few memories of Dean (I have always called my dad by his first name) killed my desire to learn about his life.

The lack of family support didn't inspire much curiosity in that direction either. Why learn about people who don't care to know about you?

You would be right in thinking that I was a blunt child. However, I learned early on to mask that part of my personality.

Adults spent much of my youth telling me I was too blunt.

## Chapter 10

## AGE 38, NYC

"Cynthia, your call with Katherine Heigl's mom is in fifteen minutes. Then you have cocktails at the Four Seasons," said one of my assistants at Escada.

I was in the process of putting the German fashion brand back on the international map. The last time they had dressed an A-list celebrity was Kim Basinger for her LA Confidential Oscar win in the late 90s.

Funny antidote: I bought Kim's pale green Oscar dress at an auction she held to raise funds for animal rights. I surprised the founders with an archive I built of their most important gowns.

Katherine was bright, fun, and had a fantastic figure. She was also very open to new ideas. After getting to know her, I made dressing her part of my growth strategy.

I was on a roll. After closing my first luxury agency to take the position, I recently dressed the stars of *Desperate Housewives* and *Sex and the City* for a slew of red-carpet events, a coup by any brand's standards.

I could not resist the free reign the CEO and German founder gave me. Nor the opportunity to work with designer Brian Rennie and his yummy couture gowns.

My success blew Mom's mind; she had watched me rise from orphanage to foster home to NYC trendsetter. She was very proud and wanted me to visit. However, she knew I was afraid to return to Memphis.

I had been running from Jimmy and a ring of men for nearly 20 years and was not about to have my past show up and ruin the life I had built for myself.

One day soon, I wish I had been brave enough to visit Memphis.

# Chapter 11

## AGE 9, THE ORPHANAGE

I was zipping through the streets. The sun shone, and I could smell black top, grass, and clean air.

"Girl, you better get to Saint Pete's before they figure out you're gone," said Mamah. I didn't know her real name. Mamah was a working girl, at least; I was pretty sure she was.

She wore colorful, tight clothing that barely contained her voluptuous figure. The size of her boobs used to fascinate me. She had to turn sideways to get down the stairs. It was something to behold. She always teased me about running around Memphis on my own.

Sometimes we would talk about life. Other times, she just wanted someone to say hello. Today, it was hello.

A few streets later, I knew I was being followed. It was starting to make me nervous. The first couple of times it happened, I thought it was someone who worked at the orphanage.

After getting a few glimpses, I knew it was several strange men. I was sensitive to people's energy, and their eyes scared me.

I cut through the side streets. I know the area well. Pretty soon, I lost them. I didn't understand why they were watching me, but it couldn't be good.

I loved being on my own. I explored every building I could. I took great satisfaction in getting into locked spaces. For some reason, it was essential to learn everything I could about the places kids weren't supposed to go.

I wanted to learn how people lived and how the world worked. So, I became adept at locks, tall gates, and high balconies. Roofs were handy.

You could learn a lot about a city by seeing it from every rooftop. I would turn each one into my playground. Every brick wall, ladder, and pipe was my gymnasium.

Years later, clients would say that I could see around corners; whenever they said this, I would think it was because I was standing on the roof.

# Chapter 12

## AGE 9, THE ORPHANAGE

Sister Anne Elizabeth and I were walking through the garden. I enjoyed our talks because she encouraged me to be myself. She didn't mind my constant questions or tendency to be blunt.

We discussed the babies she cared for at Saint Peter's.

How she handled dying infants made her the hero of my childhood.

She handled them with a love that helped me believe in a better world.

I couldn't remember the illness, but the infants had severely swollen heads and not long to live.

She gave them the attention that their families could not provide for them. She did that for all of us.

## SHAMAN ISIS

In the early 70s, it was common for parents to run from severely deformed children. She did everything she could to make their short lives beautiful.

Many kids, including sick babies, had been left on Saint Peter's doorstep. I found it strange how that experience elevated some children's circumstances over others.

Children left on the doorstep were gifted shame by a society too stupid to blame itself for how they treated each other. To some degree, we were all left on the orphanage's doorstep. Did how we were left matter?

Sister Anne Elizabeth was wonderful to all the kids, especially the sick babies. She would gently sing while rocking them in her arms.

Her eyes glowed with a healing light that I knew was rare. She may have been plain by 70s standards, especially in her black habit, but she was radiant with love. These moments are some of the most beautiful memories of my life.

I asked her why the parents abandoned their children when they knew they were dying; she explained that many adults were too fragile to handle truth or death. That made a lot of sense to me.

I watched her every chance I got. Her ability to love unconditionally was fascinating. However, it was the light that came from her head and hands that I watched the most. She was a healer. The glow reminded me of the stars in the sky.

I always wondered if she could see the same glow in me. I had been using it to help others feel better for as long as I could remember.

I wanted to tell her about the creepy men but was concerned that something would happen to her.

The children needed Sister Anne Elizabeth.

# Chapter 13

## AGE 9, THE ORPHANAGE

It was early in the day. I squeezed my skinny backside past the fence of Saint Peter's.

It was nice out, and I wanted to run around and check on my friends. There were also some run-down apartments I wanted to visit.

They were considered dangerous. That may be why somebody always propped open all the doors. Perhaps they thought if others could see in, then nothing terrible would happen. The open doors are what caught my attention in the first place.

The fact that people called the area "dangerous" was odd since Memphis was the murder capital of America. Didn't that make the whole city dangerous?

In front of one doorway, someone was braiding their hair in the sunshine. I noticed a flat iron warming in a pan on the stove.

I vaguely knew the small, thin black woman cooking in the next apartment. The stove was so close to the door that I could smell what I thought was meat.

When I looked at the pan, I realized she was cooking rats. She looked mortified that I could see what she was doing.

She said something about making sure they were dead. However, we both knew she was hungry—no one skinned rats to kill them. I didn't judge. I had seen how difficult the city was for poor people.

We exchanged gazes. The woman could feel that I understood. We smiled at each other, and I moved on.

I would never look at a rat the same again.

## Chapter 14

## AGE 9, THE ORPHANAGE

There was a building I wanted to check out. It was one of the tallest buildings around. I was determined to explore every inch of it.

I was naturally athletic. Big rooftops were perfect for gymnastic moves, and adults weren't around to tell you not to do something stupid.

I was yelled at more than once when they spotted me zipping around the city.

Roofs were my obstacle course. Sometimes, a few of the kids would join me. We turned it into a contest. Every bit of urban architecture was fair game. We would cheer each other on while simultaneously trying to top acrobatic moves.

One day, I was making my rounds when I spotted men following me again. They weren't content to watch me this time. They decided to give chase.

I could not believe I had to outrun a car. I decided to be slick and take to the side streets. That might have worked before, but the gig was up.

The next thing I know, I am trapped in an alley between them. They had gotten out of the car and followed me on foot. They could have been office buddies heading to a baseball game if it wasn't for the evil look in their eyes.

They were saying things that scared me. All I knew was that I had to get away.

I ran for the closest door. I had one advantage: I knew most of the buildings in the area.

They ran after me. I was thankful that I had learned to navigate the floors.

The men were right behind me. So, I did the only thing I could think to do. I went for the obstacle course on top. I could feel the irritation behind me. It felt like flames licking my feet.

Choosing the roof was my saving grace. They were getting confused and breathless. At one point, I hid in one of the roof depressions. My heart was pounding so hard I was struggling to hear. After the closest man passed, I ran to the other side.

I could hear them yell, "There she is." So, I went into full monkey mode. Part of me was thrilled that so many of the moves I learned from other kids came in handy. I turned one long pipe into a balance beam and backtracked to swing onto the fire escape.

Looking down, they couldn't figure out how I managed to turn the top rail into a parallel bar. I leaped. Yep, I was fearless, jumping that far from that high.

Part of me wanted to flip them off. However, I was too scared. I took the fire escape to the ground.

I remember being afraid that someone would get to the street before I did, but I was home free. I ran back to Saint Peter's.

Years later, I would hear that what the other kids and I were doing was called free-running. I found that name ironic.

# Chapter 15
## AGE 12, MOM'S

My mom had finally gotten us out of Saint Peter's for good. Mom, my sisters Deanna and Mish, and I were finally together. My sisters looked like my mom. They even had blonde hair, as she did as a child. I was the odd duck out, inches taller and with the dark looks of my father.

My youngest sister, Mish, was not thrilled to have us home. She had lived with our mom since she was a baby. The orphanage would have put her up for adoption at that age. So, they allowed Mom to take her back at six months old.

That made for a strange dynamic that would haunt our family for decades. I was resigned to the idea that Mish and Mom had a stronger bond.

Deanna, the oldest, had been displaying strange behavior for years. There was anger and bitterness in her that I didn't understand. She also resented Mish for getting to live with our mom.

Deanna liked to create fear and provoke emotion in people. I found that disturbing. Mish and I talked about how scary she could be several times.

I was nearing my teens when we finally got to live together.

We moved into a two-bedroom apartment on the outskirts of Memphis. It was much nicer than where Mom had lived before. Nearly every time I visited her, something weird happened.

One time, I accidentally burned Deanna's hand with boiling water. Why did I drink hot water? I don't know. I also had strange eating habits. I loved sugar, rock salt, and ice. I would eat the same thing for weeks if I could. My sisters teased me about it for years.

There was also a strange man with a pronounced limp. He would follow me from a distance. Something was off, as if he lacked human emotion. He tried to corner me a few times, but I had learned to stop most people in their tracks with one look.

I swear, every time I visited Mom, the sheriff's office was kicking a family out of their apartment. It was always painful to see people getting evicted.

The women would wail or yell, and the men would get angry, physical, or both. I understood they were scared.

I would have hated the deputies, but most found the task upsetting.

Unlike some of the kids at Saint Peter's, I had spent time with my mother growing up. We alternated between going home with various foster parents and our mom every few months for the weekend.

The foster parents were a mix of excellent and awful experiences. It was clear that many of them were in it for the money. The government could have given the same funds to families that couldn't afford to keep their children. That always seemed backward to me.

The sisters would freak out if they knew what happened in some of these homes.

There was a lot of drinking and some drug use. They tried to hide it, but I was always a curious child. What can I say? Exploring didn't end with buildings.

Don't get me wrong. For every awful foster family, there was a family that deserved praise. I experienced selflessness in its most authentic expression. Some couples took in countless kids and made a beautiful home out of the craziness. I admired them for that.

We were in the deep South, so many foster families were religious. That is how I would describe my central foster family, Jimmy and Shirley. They were the family we spent a lot of time with.

My older sister Deanna and I lived in separate buildings at Saint Peter's. We should have known each other better. I once got my ass-whooped by Sister Mary Rose (again!) for visiting Deanna on my own.

I was trying to converse with Deanna when one of the kids ran in and said, "They are coming for you." Deanna came to life for a moment. She seemed disinterested in my visit and happy I was in deep crap. The sparkle that suddenly came into her eyes bothered me for years.

They took me from the room by my ear. I knew I was about to get a hell of a whooping. I didn't understand why they were so upset with me. Then I realized it was one thing to disappear and reappear; it was another to break the rules in front of other staff.

Sister Mary Rose went off on me. My ear was burning, and my backside was about to burn worse. She could be ruthless with her words and hands.

She took immense pleasure in beating the shit out of me. I had bruises on my legs and backside. Part of me wanted to tell the other sisters what she did when she got to take her anger out on the kids. In those days, children rarely ratted out adults because nobody believed them. Sad, but true.

So, Deanna and I spent time together when we visited Mom or when Jimmy and Shirley took us both for a visit. That was a few times a year. They were the foster parents who remained a part of our lives after we moved in with our mom.

I'm glad Deanna and I started seeing Shirley and Jimmy independently, as she acted weird whenever we visited them.

She was both jealous and oddly protective. One day, it all makes sense.

# Chapter 16

## AGE 29, NYC

My new job in public relations was wild. After a few years working in the eyewear industry, I landed a position with *New York Post* editor Richard Johnson's wife, Nadine Johnson. She was the go-to for society and fashion events.

Nadine could be challenging, but *The New York Times* writer who introduced us told me that if I could last a year, I could write my ticket in the industry. I was determined to stay a year. She was a striking, tall, blond woman with a thick Belgian-French accent.

Within a few days of starting, things happened that surprised me. First, my office mate, Bridget, informed me that a real-life princess had recently vacated my new desk. I thought princesses were rare.

I have taken her old job. My predecessor had up and married the duty-free king and left to be a full-time princess.

I was given Studio 54 icon Ian Schrager's new project as my first client. Studio 54 was the world's most famous nightclub. Infamous for drug and celebrity antics. I could not believe I was going to get to work with him.

Next, Nadine asked me if I would be responsible for the PR for an upcoming event. I took the binder she was holding and turned it around. The cover said Azzedine Alaia & Andy Warhol Retrospective at the Guggenheim Museum.

My first thought was, shit. During our interview, Nadine asked if I knew how to use Microsoft Word and Excel, and I answered yes. I barely knew how to use email.

I spent the next week figuring out how to use both programs.

This event would set the tone for some of the most impactful years of my life. I worked hard to build a reputation in eyewear to leap into PR. I had patiently waited for my dream manifestations to come true.

Holding that binder, I knew all my work was about to pay off.

# Chapter 17

## AGE 29, NYC

I was heading to The Globe to handle an opening night event for the UK's *Tatler* magazine, the *Town & Country* of Britain. The restaurant's owners were thrilled with the event.

The *Entertainment Tonight* crew met me to interview the party's main attraction, President Bush's niece, Lauren Bush. Lauren was a beautiful young woman with impeccable manners. I liked her immediately.

The party was her coming out to New York Society. She wore an American flag on the magazine's cover. It was a nod of support post 9/11. I thought that was cool.

I liked the whole Bush family. Lauren and her mother, Sharon, were lovely. Neil Bush was very respectful.

My instincts said that their marriage was about to come apart. I don't know what gave it away, but I was rarely wrong.

My powerful intuition and visions kept me safe many times and came in handy in my career.

The Secret Service was already in-house. The guest list was a who's who of the literary world.

I worked with the Secret Service on a few events. I admit it was exciting.

One of my favorite parts of working in high-end PR is the fascinating people.

I spent a day with Marilyn Monroe's former husband, Arthur Miller, spoke in depth with iconic author Tom Wolfe, worked with *Vogue* magazine's Anna Wintour many times, and met Bill and Hillary Clinton at fundraisers I secured for clients.

Arthur Miller asked me to ensure that no one brought up Marilyn Monroe. The wound was still bleeding. I found that sad.

I liked working with the Secret Service. They have seen it all. When they looked into my eyes, It reminded me of how I scanned people to know if they were trustworthy. I passed muster.

SHAMAN ISIS

At first, I was worried they would ask me about my past. Thank God I have a new legal name. It might have gone differently if I still used one of my aliases.

I had decided not to party at this event. Ever since 9/11, I have noticed an uptick in my drinking. I had never been much of a drinker. I did not want to start now.

## Chapter 18

### AGE 26, NYC

Working for Robert Marc taught me a lot. I got a job with the eyewear guru shortly after arriving in NYC. His attention to detail and customer service allowed me to build quite a list of clients. I still had difficulty believing I had customers like Steve Jobs, Sigourney Weaver, and Marc Anthony.

These days, I use the name Cynthia Lucci. People often asked me if I was related to Susan. I thought that was funny.

The clients who came to Robert's stores for advice were legendary. During my first week, Yoko Ono and Michael Douglas popped in for a fitting.

I spent the first couple of years working in Robert's flagship on 57th and Madison, learning at the feet of some of the most influential people in the world. Names that regularly appear in all the newspapers.

My confidence took a giant leap as I learned to advise important people on what they should wear. I was always frank but had learned to wield it with sophistication.

Once I tamed my southern accent, I handled media, VIPs, and eyewear trend stories.

One of my favorite people to work with was the founder of New York Fashion Week, Fern Mallis. She took risks with her eyewear choices and was always game to test the newest designs.

I had learned enough about the optical world to create original lens cuts and colors for the stores that would do well with fashion media.

She has been coming in for a while. I was pleasantly surprised one day when she offered to give me a reference. She had noticed the press that my funky lenses were generating. I will soon take her up on the offer.

My next client of the day was quite a character. His name was Alvan Navaro. He always wore a white suit with a Panama hat. He ran for President of Ecuador.

He had been coming to see me for a while.

One of the businesses he owned was the Bonita banana company. He would send a Lincoln SUV with a few boxes of bananas every few months.

I shared gifts from my clients with everyone in the company. The bananas led to some serious teasing. I would place them in the eyewear trays the messengers carried from the lab to the stores. Jokes ensued.

Lately, I had felt he wanted to speak to me about something. Instead, Mr. Navaro's right-hand man showed up for his appointment. I always thought of him as his head of security. He had that look in his eyes.

I just rolled with it. He was there to pick up Mr. Navaro's order. We sat at one of Robert's beautiful antique tables. I was getting a strange vibe from him.

That is when he said he came to speak to me about something. He explained that they knew I was not from NYC and may need to learn how things worked.

He said that Mr. Navaro wanted to take care of me. He explained that one of the things Mr. Navaro found appealing was my innocence. I was curious to know if they were seeing the whole picture.

"I am here to make you an offer. If you would be willing to spend a year of your life as his companion, you can pick out the apartment of your dreams overlooking Central Park. At the end of the year, you get to keep the apartment and receive enough money to set yourself up for life," he said. The amount he mentioned took my breath away.

My face was on fire, and my heart dropped to the floor. What kind of woman did they think I was?

"He wanted to make this offer before you got married. We realize that because you aren't from here, you may not know how many women go on to live a dream life after such an opportunity," he added.

I was so shocked by the turn of this conversation that I became speechless. My ears were bright red.

He continued for some time, but I couldn't hear him; I was torn between feeling complemented and pissed off.

After he left, I told my boss and good friend Jamie about the conversation. He had seen and heard it all in his day. It wasn't the first time someone powerful made an overture at me.

Flowers and gifts surprised me on several occasions. However, it was the first time someone came out, offered to "take care of me," and provided explicit details about the expectations.

Jamie had been around the block and was not quick to dismiss the opportunity. He advised me to consider it seriously as it would set me up for life. Jamie explained that people often married for the same reason and that this was a better and faster way to elevate my life. He said there is nothing wrong with an understanding between adults and that I shouldn't be so naive as to get angry about it.

So, that night, I gave it some thought. First, I had to tell myself to grow up and look at it from a worldly viewpoint. I couldn't hold that for long. It just sounded like glorified prostitution to me.

When he came to see me again, I said something like thank you, but I couldn't do it. Please tell Mr. Navaro how flattered I am. Mr. Navaro was not happy. He stopped coming to see me not long after that.

Years later, I would listen to the radio, and Jay Leno shared a story about hooking up with a model in her apartment overlooking Central Park. He said it was the middle of the night, and he was starving, but because of her job, there was no food in the kitchen. He explained that he spotted boxes of bananas and decided to eat a banana. When he looked inside, the boxes were full of automatic weapons.

All I could think was, "If true, that was a close call."

Soon afterward, I got to take Fern up on her offer and secure my career in PR. She would become my fashion fairy godmother, a nickname I gave her in the late 90s.

## Chapter 19

### Age 7, Memphis

The vision came over me again. I was in bed at Saint Peter's when I came awake scared. In my mind's eye, I had seen the men coming through the doors again. They were up to no good. I learned from experience that these were intuitive visions.

We didn't have much time.

I roused the kids nearest me. We had to be quick and quiet. The worst thing that could happen was getting caught.

I used my eyes to give directions to two of the other kids. We were so adept at this that I knew we talked without words.

Saint Peter's was enormous, so hiding was easy. This time, we snuck into the bathroom and climbed into the tubs elevated off the ground. The height made it easier for the sisters to bathe the younger children.

We laid down in the tubs and stayed there until they were gone. I don't know how I knew they were gone; I just did. We would sneak back to our beds and go back to sleep.

I was scared that the men knew about my visions. I wondered if this was one of the reasons people followed me. It was all very confusing.

The other kids and I never talked about it. Somehow, we knew that bringing up late-night visits was dangerous.

One day, when I finally decided to share my truth, I would ask myself if I should bring it up. I worried that I would rouse memories that may be best left alone. I finally accepted two things: my detailed memories were unusual, and I had to speak my truth.

# Chapter 20

## Age 12, Memphis

The first summer we moved in together as a family was pretty awesome. I lived in the apartment complex pool and learned to play most sports with the other kids. We watched each other's backs.

There were a lot of fights with neighboring gangs.

My sisters were small, blond, and pretty. That became the number one reason I got into fights with boys. I was becoming something of a brawler.

Unfortunately, my sister Deanna was named Dolly D. She was petite but top-heavy. Her figure caused many issues with boys. I was much taller than both sisters, a bean pole.

I loved rollerskating more than anything. I also still loved rooftops.

Soon after moving, I turned the roof of our building into my private nest. I would go up there to read, tan, and watch the stars.

I liked to think about space. I asked myself existential questions that turned my brain to mush. How were we created? Are there aliens? Why was Earth the only planet with life on it? Did God exist? Yep, I nearly drove myself crazy.

I would visit places I wasn't supposed to see. The entire complex became my playground, including the woods next door.

On occasion, I would get into crazy situations.

A massive panel in the breezeway housed the wiring for phones and electricity. I unlocked it to see the power arching between two pads. I found electricity fascinating.

One time, I got a little too curious. I was playing with the current. I just wanted to see how it reacted to different types of interference.

I decided to try the pencil behind my ear. That did not go well. My hand became fused as soon as I stuck it in the middle of the arc.

I could feel electricity powering through my entire body. My hair was doing strange things. Finally, I heard a loud pop, and all the power went out in the area.

Well, thank God I was free! Albeit, I felt strange for a couple of days.

As my sixth grade year rounded the corner, I became excited. I was fully expecting my new school to be fun.

That is not what happened.

# Chapter 21

## AGE 12, MOM'S

In the first week of sixth grade, I became the target of some of the most popular girls.

They heard one of the boys say something nice to me, and that was all it took. I had always liked to hang out with boys. They didn't mind my bluntness or love of athletics.

I grew up with boys and girls playing together. Barbie dolls were not something I remember at Saint Peter's. These were Barbie girls.

They hated me within my first two days. Deanna was no help. She was a teenager in middle school. We weren't even in the same building (again!).

By the end of the week, they were ganging up on me. I was a fighter, but there were too many of them. On top of that, I was not used to being in school. I just wanted to fly under the radar, and they were making that impossible.

By the second week, they stopped me every chance they got to pinch, kick and punch. They were a wall of hate I did not know how to handle. They had everyone afraid to even get near me. I was toxic. No one wanted to piss off Mercy and her little gang of angry pre-teens.

The teacher knew what was happening, but these kids had grown up in the area. Their parents were involved and local. My mom worked nights and slept days.

The situation became severe; they were attacking me almost every day. I didn't understand why they hated me so much.

That started me down a road that would end spectacularly.

I came home and cried in the bathroom for the first few months. I wanted to tell my mother but knew that would be a waste of time. I wasn't the only girl they picked on, and I had seen how well things went for the girls whose parents complained. It was useless.

Months after it started, I saw my tear-stained, snot-nosed face in the bathroom mirror. I immediately stopped crying. Feeling sorry for myself was not helping. I was sick of getting my ass kicked by a bunch of awful girls.

So, I sat down and thought about it. I realized that I had to do something extreme.

Finally, I used some of the skills I had learned at Saint Peter's.

I followed them. I studied them like the enemy they were. I watched their personal lives. I checked out their parents and homes. I inspected them like the buildings I played in a few years ago.

Once I understood the landscape, I went after each of them while they were alone.

The only warning they received was the karma-is-a-bitch look on my face.

I will be frank. I beat the ever-loving shit out of every one of my tormentors. It's terrible, but I enjoyed it more than it is probably healthy.

I was taking back my life.

The next time I went to school, people moved away when I walked through the hallways. They whispered about me. I suddenly had a reputation for being a bad girl.

Okay, who cared? It's not like I was learning anything useful.

MTV had just come out. The world was changing. I wanted to dance, sing, and go to concerts. I wanted to say fuck you to them all.

I started skipping classes to hang out with an older crowd. I always preferred older people.

I also made a new friend. Her name was Tanoa; she was so tiny that she reminded me of a bird. She lived in a massive log cabin near the school.

We became best friends through 7th grade. We smoked pot and watched indie movies like *Cheech and Chong* on one of the first beta maxes.

When a friend had a birthday party, I drank too many beers and smoked so much pot that I fell asleep for a whole day. When I woke up, Tanoa told me my mom had called the police and reported me as a runaway.

I didn't understand why my mom did something so extreme.

Sure, she was confused about why I was getting into fights and listening to rock music, but I didn't think I deserved that punishment. I was 13 and in a shit load of trouble.

It would be a while before her decision made sense.

When I got home, she told me that if I got in trouble again, she would have the police come and pick me up for "running away." I couldn't tell her what had happened.

I was always careful to skip classes with teachers who didn't care. Several teachers were so drunk during the day that I doubt they even noticed. Aside from falling asleep for a long time after that party, I couldn't understand why she was so concerned.

When Deanna and I discussed it, I was surprised at her behavior. She was cold and far too satisfied that I was in so much trouble.

For a moment, I thought it was because she cared, but that wasn't quite the truth. She had much bigger fish to fry than a sister suddenly getting Mom's attention.

My intuition has never come in that handy with the people closest to me.

When I returned to school, the principal called me to his office to inform me that I would be suspended from every school in the district. The school board thought they were helping me by kicking me out of the school system.

I had no idea that someone had gone to them with lies. Betrayal leaves a lasting taste.

When I got home, my mother called the police to pick me up for running away from home. She acted like she was doing me a favor.

That is how I spent time in juvie with teens who had committed serious crimes like murder. In those days, runaways were criminals. No one asked why you were acting out.

The black policewoman who picked me up had seen it all. As she drove downtown, I accepted where she was taking me. I decided to check my purse. Oops, I had contraband. So, I asked her to throw my Zig-Zag papers out the window. She just rolled her eyes.

Juvie turned out to be a prison for young people. I was surprised at how high-tech it was. Nothing on TV looked anything like this place.

They booked, photographed, and strip-searched me like a hardened criminal. Next up was a thick concrete cell. My new prison had a cement block bed, toilet, sink, steel door, and a thin window strip along one ceiling.

I would brace myself high on the walls to peek out the hand-size window. I needed to see the grass and feel the sunshine.

I had been using the sun to recharge my energy my whole life.

## Chapter 22

## AGE 13, MEMPHIS

After some time, they sent me to a halfway house. It was a rambling old place near the prison. Soon after I arrived, my mom and younger sister came to visit.

It was an awkward affair. Mom kept apologizing for not realizing they would lock me up for a while. I didn't tell her about the cell or being strip-searched. She was already radiating so much anxiety. They didn't stay long. I didn't blame them.

My close friends wanted to rant about her decision. I knew my mom; something was off. The things she was alluding to didn't fit.

I tried to leave the halfway house to see my old haunts in Memphis. I wanted something to cheer me up. I wanted to run on the rooftops.

A vehicle started following me. When I finally got a good look, I realized the creeps were back. They had the same equipment and energy as those who followed me at Saint Peter's.

I turned around and went back to the halfway house. I needed to get back to our apartment.

It wasn't long after I returned home that the other shoe dropped; Deanna was 14 and pregnant.

Mom sat me down to explain what had been going on. Before she learned about the pregnancy, Deanna had come to her to express her concerns about me. She also visited the principal of my school. The things she told both were outright lies.

I was still a virgin. I had never even seen hard drugs. My friends were not junkies, and I was not hanging out in drug dens. My face was so red that my mother had to realize I was angry.

She didn't know what she was going to do. She did explain that I had the potential to be anything I wanted to be. She didn't want me to waste my life.

She explained that she was trying to save me, even if it didn't seem that way. Deep down, she knew what Deanna had done and wanted to get me out of town.

Not long before all this happened, Mom had seen a psychic who predicted my older sister had something important to tell her.

The woman also told my mom that she needed to get me somewhere I could get a decent education and time around normal kids. She said many things that became true.

A few days later, I came home to find my foster mom, Shirley, sitting on the couch in our living room. It might as well have been Jesus for the reaction it got out of me. I immediately knew what was about to happen.

My mother once called Shirley homely. I thought she just needed better hair and makeup. She was a pear-shaped woman with short reddish-brown hair and glittering blue eyes. She was allergic to everything. So, by 80s standards, her lack of poof and makeup made her vanilla.

I could tell she was there for a serious talk. She told me that Mom was on the verge of a nervous breakdown. The scandal of a 14-year-old pregnant daughter was the kind of thing that wrecked futures.

While listening to Shirley, my best friend Tanoa was waiting outside. She had gotten a special driving permit called a hardship license and a bright yellow Pontiac Firebird for her birthday. We were going to celebrate over the coming days.

I ran down to tell her I would be visiting my foster parents. I didn't have the heart to tell her what I suspected. She nodded her bottle-blond head and shrugged her tiny shoulders. Sad that I wouldn't be with her for her birthday in a few days.

## Chapter 23

## AGE 14, COLLIERVILLE

I was doing one of my favorite things: bathing. Bathrooms are one of the few places where you can have privacy.

My sisters and I used to fight over the sink and mirror. I would perch Indian-style on the sink to do my makeup. I have always loved makeup.

I was relaxing in a nice bathtub on the second floor of Shirley and Jimmy's suburban home. They had moved to an expensive area outside of Memphis called Collierville.

I was thinking about everything that had happened. Tubs are good for thinking. My wardship had recently been assigned to my foster parents. The whole experience was surreal.

Suddenly, I knew I was being observed. I didn't react at first. I waited until I figured out how I was being watched. I could feel the energy coming from above me.

Finally, I spotted a small hole in the ceiling above the tub. Suddenly, the light shifted, and I knew I was right.

Well, shit, this development was not good. Only one person could make and use a hole in the attic: my foster father, Jimmy.

Soon after arriving, they told me I was visiting for the summer. I couldn't believe that any more than I had a line about my short visit.

After that, Jimmy took me to get the rest of my clothes from my mom's. They were unhappy with my parachute pants, boots, and zippered tops.

On returning to their house, I became very nervous around Jimmy. He had been looking at me in a way that freaked me out.

On the way back to his house, he brought up sex. I was shocked. They were both very religious. This one-sided conversation was disgusting.

He kept looking at me. His glassy blue eyes widened with excitement at his bad behavior. The overly tan scalp that dominated his combover gleamed in the dashboard lights.

I will never forget how he repeatedly said, "It wasn't the size of the wave, but the motion of the ocean." He was trying to get a 13-year-old girl he had known since childhood to have a gross conversation. It left me sad and scared. How would he not take advantage of me living in his house?

All I could do was squeeze myself against the car door and wonder if I would have to jump out of another moving vehicle. I thought, dammit, it's dark out.

When he realized I was unhappy with the chat, he reminded me that as long as I was good, they wouldn't send me away to the school for bad girls. I had been hearing about this school for years. It was a prison school for young women that society couldn't handle.

My friends and I heard horrible things about the place. It was a terrifying threat, especially after spending time in juvie.

The night I brought the rest of my clothes to their house, Shirley sat me down to explain how it would be in their home. She was going to put me to work cleaning and cooking.

First, we needed to have a ritual. Shirley caressed her Bible as she stated that my evil spirit had infected their house. She went on about how the women of my family had bad blood. That we couldn't help but sin. She had always been religious in the extreme, but I found her words hurtful.

As far as I knew, she had never seen my sin. Why was she bashing all the women in my family? She had grown up with a silver spoon in her mouth. She didn't know the first thing about real life. Deanna's pregnancy and my "running away" from home were examples of what lousy stock we were.

Finally, she got to the point. We were going to perform a religious ritual. She brought out a candle and a second bible. She gave me the lit candle and one of the Bibles and then took me into every room to pray for my evil soul out of the house. Apparently, "it" had infected every nook and cranny.

I thought the prayer she had me repeat was horrible. Forcing me to my knees in every room seemed to thrill her. I could feel Jimmy watching us make our way through the house.

I could only think that evil comes in many forms, sometimes wearing a cross.

As she recited my lines, I prayed, "Lord, let me survive these two looney birds long enough to reach adulthood."

I wanted to scream at her that her husband was a pervert, but I thought she might already know based on her behavior.

## MEMORY MANSION

The bathtub peephole began the terror he brought to my teen years. He became obsessed. I would find holes in the house and fill them with paper, glue, or toothpaste.

He was watching me all the time. It would only get more bizarre from there.

# Chapter 24

## AGE 30, NYC

My marquee PR client, Brasserie 8 ½, was a massive success. Real estate magnate Sheldon Solow owned the stunning restaurant. Sheldon was a distinguished silver-haired man who wore beautiful suits.

He was delighted with the events and publicity I had secured.

He built the stunning restaurant to house his wall-sized Leger and Matisse artwork. He had an excellent taste in art. No surprise for a man who owned the iconic 9 West 57th Street skyscraper.

I was delighted to get to work with such a dynamic man. He trusted me with his baby, 8 ½. We would discuss the restaurant, his dream customer, and his pet project—a development near the rail yards.

I descended the restaurant's famous orange spiral staircase in my designer heels and fashion-forward outfit to have lunch with Anna Wintour. We were doing a tasting and going over a Vogue magazine event coming up in April. I was delighted she trusted me to be there when her event head was on maternity leave.

This event was my crowning achievement for 8 ½. It was a premiere of the film *Moulin Rouge*, benefiting the CFDA. I was getting to work with Anna, the director Baz Lurhman, and his incredibly talented wife, Catherine Martin.

Top designers worldwide have created one-of-a-kind *Moulin Rouge*-themed dresses to be auctioned off by an upcoming actor named Hugh Jackman.

The top models in the world would walk a custom-built stage we were constructing. The guest list was a big deal. My boss, Nadine, already told me she was coming whether Anna liked it. Nadine was happy that I had booked a slew of events with *Vogue*. She was annoyed not to have already been invited to the big event.

Chef Julian Alonzo, one of my favorite chefs, was excited about the tasting. Anna arrived with her boyfriend, Shelby. He was a bit of a flirt but harmless. We went over the event and sampled the food. She was pleased with the table arrangements and menu we prepared.

Nicole Kidman was coming to the event. She had a massive moment in the media as she got a divorce, and the rumor mill pushed the event into overdrive.

I worked directly with Anna several times. I found her to be very interesting. She was direct but kind. I was never on the receiving end of "Nuclear Wintour."

The night of the event was wild. The gigantic restaurant was buzzing with activity. The press lined up outside as though The Academy Awards were taking place.

This event was more significant than the anniversary party I worked on for Giorgio Armani. The party was a star-studded affair and the first time I got to work with Robert Isabell.

Robert was Anna's go-to for event decor. He was a genius. He once stacked Studio 54 with so much glitter on New Year's Eve that it floated out of the walls decades later.

We always got along well. That night, we had our only tiff. He wanted to change the order and arrangement of the food and dinnerware. He was being adamant. I had my reasons.

He dragged Anna into the debate. She listened to both of us and told him to do what I had planned. She understood my thinking. Robert seemed slightly annoyed and impressed.

I was speechless. Anna wasn't even offended by my passionate explanation.

The security was very tight. The only request Sheldon made was that he meet Nicole Kidman. That seemed a tame request for the man who owned the building. I always liked that he acted like an average person for a billionaire.

Kidman was even more beautiful in person. Her skin glowed like it was lit with white light. She was incredibly gracious all night, and Sheldon was delighted to meet her.

I spent the evening ensuring everything was perfect and dealing with the ongoing security issue. You would be amazed at how many people try to break into events mentioned in the media. Anna also had a slew of haters.

# Chapter 25

## AGE 30, NYC

I worked on events for Sean "Puff Daddy" Coombs, Jennifer "JLo" Lopez, George Clooney, Miramax, HBO, and others that year. I developed excellent working relationships with the folks at Miramax and HBO.

One night at dinner, two guys who had worked for Miramax warned me never to be alone with Harvey Weinstein.

That was not the first time I was warned about him. It was the first time men warned me. I knew the second I met Weinstein that he had something in common with my foster father. He got the cold but professional version of me.

I was an adept actress. I have been acting, in fact, masking, for decades. I had a closet full of personalities I could pull on like suits. I did a great ice queen.

I was careful never to give anyone the idea that I was a social climber.

I shared a few stories about my PR work at dinner that night. That conversation would have mind-blowing consequences for my career. They took my anecdotes back to the team at *Sex and the City*. The next thing I knew, we did five episodes with my stories and clients in the script.

It was a big deal. The show was an enormous success. I negotiated hard. I should have asked for credit but prioritized getting the clients named and featured in the script.

Many restaurants and clubs were in the background of SATC episodes; few were mentioned in the script, especially on the scale I manifested.

Bungalow 8 was getting an entire episode. When we first launched Amy Sacco's iconic nightclub, we sent fancy black key cards to over 200 people, the cream of NYC nightlife. The exclusivity of that type of launch became the storyline for one episode.

I was also delighted that Brasserie 8 ½ was in a special episode featuring the fashion industry. On the day of filming, Sheldon was delighted to bring his son over to meet

Sarah Jessica Parker. I had met her before, but this was the first time we had coffee together.

When the *Sex and the City* crew discovered that Sheldon was coming by with his son, they brought a signed director's chair as a surprise gift.

Father and son were delighted. Sheldon was clearly in love with his son. I had never seen him look so happy.

In the opening scene, Sarah Jessica Parker's character "Carrie" says Brasserie 8 ½ was the place to see and be seen. The camera showcased the gorgeous orange spiral staircase, bar, and restaurant.

Margaret Cho, Sarah, and Willie Garson did a fantastic scene about the superficiality of appearance.

Sarah's character would also fall while walking the runway at a fashion show. I knew these two cultural moments would be a huge PR coup.

After the episode aired, you could not get another person inside the massive restaurant.

The events, press, and episodes from the hottest show in the world were such a big deal that the management company asked me to consult on a slew of NYC landmarks. My new list of clients included the Rockefeller Center, Lincoln Center, and The World Trade Center.

I was thrilled. Landing that portfolio of clients meant that I would be able to open an agency shortly.

## MEMORY MANSION

The management company asked me to "8 ½" the World Trade Center. They wanted the famous building and rooftop restaurant to be just as hot.

My mother did not know what to think of my success in NYC.

I did; I had dreamed big and worked my ass off—two critical ingredients in manifesting.

# Chapter 26

## AGE 14, COLLIERVILLE

I liked Collierville, the suburb I live in these days. It is a beautiful town. The people seemed friendly.

That helped me deal with the craziness in my home life. Jimmy had turned my guardianship into a nightmare.

He watched me all the time. The peepholes became something I worked around. I got tired of filling them up only to find new ones later. I figured out how to get dressed without being easy to see.

During the day, I cleaned, read, prayed, and accompanied Shirley to church and charitable work. We did everything from teaching bible study in underprivileged areas to giving motion therapy to sick children and helping at special education schools.

It would have been far more enjoyable if her religious beliefs were not so rigid. I was forever getting lectured on how to be a good wife and woman. The Bible is a frequent reference.

Sometimes, we would argue about the verses she would quote. I couldn't help myself. I would point out passages that contradicted her verses. She would get very annoyed.

Not long after arriving, she told me I better not complain about her husband as many other young girls had. She emphasized that the girl's unfortunate background caused them to make up lies.

The ironic part is she helped me out. As she shared their stories, I tucked away the details. These details prepared me for what Jimmy would try to do.

The conversation was confirmation that she knew her husband was sick. She also admitted the girls had been taken care of for "lying" about her husband.

This conversation made me realize that I must handle the situation alone.

The way he looked at me made my skin crawl. He was always trying to find an excuse to hug or kiss me. A few weeks after moving in, I found him trying to sneak into my room at night.

I had never slept well, a hangover from my days at Saint Peter's. That came in handy with his late-night visits.

Over the summer, I would wake to find him standing over my bed. The look on his face was frightening. Seeing his surprise when I woke up every time made me feel some sense of control.

He thought being silent would help. He didn't realize that I felt his energy enter the room. That is what woke me up—the vibration of evil.

He got so close a few times I could feel the covers being pulled back. My eyes would snap open, and I would ask him the question I did every time this happened, "what do you want?"

He would pretend he was there to check on me. We both knew that was a lie.

One day, months later, he tried to attack me in the attic. He is lucky that I didn't kill him. I wanted to shove him back down the staircase. Instead, we struggled, and I pushed him very hard.

He started whining. He said he couldn't help himself. At the same time, he brought up the girl's prison.

We went back and forth until I finally said we would both go to prison. I added that I would gladly go to the prison for girls after telling everyone what a pig he was.

He begged for my forgiveness. I thought this would bring an end to my nightmare.

# MEMORY MANSION

He only became more obsessed and controlling.

## Chapter 27

## AGE 50, 2020

I was no longer hungry. I suddenly stopped caring about the work I had been doing for decades. I was beyond exhausted and no longer had the energy to pretend.

I wanted to use my real name. I needed to speak the truth. I no longer wanted to wear a mask and live in shame and regret.

I wanted to set the world on fire. My anger was finally coming to the surface. I had been running for decades. I was done running.

It felt like I was resting on the bottom of the ocean. The rays of sunlight were reaching my skin. I could feel the warmth.

# MEMORY MANSION

God, I needed to breathe. I began to kick for the surface. My legs felt heavy. My heart was burning for oxygen.

I could see a dragon in my mind's eye. It swooped down to scorch the Earth. It gave me the strength to keep swimming.

When I finally surfaced, it felt like the sun would burn my skin. It had been so long since the real me had seen daylight.

I sat on my porch. My eyes began to rotate in a rectangle - left, up, right, down, left, up, right, down, which went on for days.

I knew what was happening. I was opening memory mansion—the place where I had stored all of my good and bad experiences.

I began to feel alive again, angry but alive.

Finally, I reached up and ripped all the boxes from the rooms in my mansion. I knocked the shelves off the walls. The meticulously labeled and stored memories fell all around me.

I was surrounded by boxes full of everything I had never discussed.

That is when I finally opened my mouth and began to speak.

# Chapter 28

## AGE 23, SAN DIEGO

It was Christmas time. I found California a little sad during the holidays. People didn't decorate as they did in Tennessee. The important thing was I was safe.

After realizing the men had found me in San Diego, I disappeared from my apartment with a small bag. I packed it quickly and snuck out through a neighbor's apartment. I had not stopped shaking for days. I climbed down their second-floor balcony and dropped to the ground.

I wasn't taking any chances. I needed to disappear into the city while I figured out what to do.

I didn't care about all my stuff. I was going to get out of San Diego soon.

I hid with some Navy Seals families. I didn't need to tell them that I was in trouble. It was hard to hide my fear from people who had seen it all.

I hiked and spent time with them and their friends. Over the holidays, they let me stay in an apartment while one couple was visiting family up North.

I watched a new TV show called *Friends*. The show made me laugh at a time when I needed humor. It took place in NYC. The synchronicity confirmed where I was running next.

I always knew I would end up there.

My agent, Nancy, asked me if I wanted to move in with her for a bit. I snapped up the chance to live near the beach while figuring out how I would get out of town.

The other roommate, Sally, had a poster of a new film called *Pulp Fiction* hanging behind the sofa. I loved the movie. All the cast had signed the poster. I thought that was cool. It was donated for a fundraiser she worked on each year.

Nancy was a voluptuous brunette with tilted eyes. Her dad was in oil. She graduated with the Egyptian pyramids as her backdrop. Her ex was a local rocker in a heavy metal band. He popped by wherever he could. They were close.

Sally was a red-haired half mad gypsy. She was disabled and counted on her erratic Springer Spaniel for company.

Her wild social life and connections got us into incredible LA parties.

We would go to the coffee shop near the house to listen to live music. I loved listening to one of the girls who played there. Her name was Jewel.

According to Sally, she had told some of her friends in the music industry about Jewel. I taped her music and listened to it for weeks on end. I have always listened to my favorite songs on repeat.

Not long after moving, I was in my room reading. The hair on my body stood on end. I suddenly knew that someone was watching. I had been feeling like that for several days.

My intuition said that it was coming from the house next door. That didn't make sense because the couple that lived there were ancient and stationery.

I could not shake the feeling of being watched.

That night, I went to bed thinking I was being sensitive because of my history. Hours later, I woke up in terror. I knew before cracking my eyes that someone had opened my window. When I looked up, I saw a man climbing through.

I shot out of bed and tried to get the door open. I was shaking so badly that I couldn't turn the knob. It just kept spinning. Finally, I jerked it open and ran straight to Nancy's room.

She knew before she opened the door that something terrible was happening. I was screaming. I couldn't even hear myself.

We called the police and one of the surfers we knew. I called him Tool because Nancy played the band's music every time he stayed the night.

He arrived before the police, holding a spear gun. He was dead serious. It made us laugh for a moment.

The police should have checked the perimeter. They asked if we had been out partying that night. The funky decor made them think it was a party house. They said that something important was going on somewhere else. They were too busy to take the call seriously.

This moment was challenging for me. I became angry. I hadn't wanted to call for help because I feared being discovered. Now, it turned out the police thought it was our imagination.

After they left, we checked outside the house to find my window open and the screen resting on the ground.

Nancy and Tool offered to sleep in my room. I was shaking so severely that I struggled to get back to sleep.

An hour or so later, I heard screaming. I ran to my room and opened the door in time to see Tool running toward my window. A strange man was racing to climb out.

Tool was angry and yelling as he chased after him with the spear gun. I couldn't believe he was going after the man.

We ran to the front door. When we got outside, Tool yelled, "Where did he go?" He looked freaked out. He kept asking how the bastard could have disappeared so fast.

This experience would remind me to listen to my intuition.

The following day, Nancy and I decided to get some coffee. We were both shaken. When we got outside, there was a man in front of the door of our elderly neighbor's house. As soon as I saw his eyes, I knew it was the man who had broken into my room twice in one night.

When we returned to the house, I felt he was gone. We found out that he was the nephew of the older couple. He was running from the police. They were searching for him back home.

His parents talked the old couple into letting him hide in their house. The room he was in was right across from my window.

That was it for me. I couldn't take much more. I sold everything and ran to New York City. I had just enough money. I will find a job as soon as I arrive.

Nothing was going to stop me from being happy and prosperous.

## Chapter 29

## AGE 25, NEW YORK

The first time I came out of the subway in NYC, I was home. I have always felt very uncomfortable in Tennessee. I thought and walked fast; if I knew you, I could chatter. I was out of sync in the South. New York felt natural.

The hum and energy of the city were exciting. I found a place in New Jersey. I was close to the Path Train to Manhattan. That allowed me to visit the city. I was already booking some modeling jobs. It was fast money.

I had arrived with a couple of hundred dollars to my name. I knew that I was meant to be in New York. So, I was okay. I was manifesting the career of my dreams.

In the airport in San Diego, I saw a beautiful woman wearing a suit and walking confidently. People looked at her with respect. I told myself that someday, I would be treated that way.

I worked at a lingerie store while I searched for jobs in NYC. I knew my lack of a degree was going to require creativity. I just needed the right opportunity.

A few weeks later, I got an interview with an eyewear guru to the stars. His name was Robert Marc. I wore my best (and only!) suit and a big smile. I got the job.

My appearance was sophisticated. My attitude and accent needed a lot of work. I commuted through the World Trade Center daily via the Path Train.

Soon after starting my new job, I became a top salesperson at the company. Robert's stores were the definition of high-end; exclusive handmade imports, a door buzzer, marble floors, Italian light fixtures, and antique tables made it the place for expensive eyewear.

I worked out of the flagship store on the corner of Madison and 57th Street, across from the LVMH Building.

Robert Marc is the person who created the concept for the luxury eyewear boutique you see all over the country nowadays.

His customer base was the most famous people across every influential industry. I have landed the perfect job that allowed me to learn from incredibly successful people. This is when I started to think about influencer marketing, an industry I would create in a couple of years.

Styling and fitting eyewear is an intimate and time-consuming business, which allowed me to have long conversations with some of the most fascinating people in the world. I soaked up everything.

I was happy, safe, and flourishing.

# Chapter 30

## AGE 13, MOM'S

The roof of our apartment building was my treehouse. My family lived on the top floor. That made it easy for me to use our balcony or the window outside our front door to climb onto the roof.

Almost every day, I would grip the slant, raise my leg, and use my toes and hands to pull my body onto the edge. I admit it was perilous, but I was fearless.

The very top of the roof was flat, which allowed me some privacy. I would take a book, towel, and beverage and stay for hours.

I loved the freedom of my treehouse. My mom and sisters weren't about to follow me up. That is how I would sneak out to explore, see friends, and check out other apartments.

I had seen the roof of almost every apartment building in the complex. I would drop into balconies and see how other people lived. I didn't think of it as breaking in. I thought of it as learning about families. I never went through their things or took anything from their homes. I just soaked in energy. Was it a happy home? Was it a sad home?

My treehouse was freedom. During the day, I would read, tan, think, and watch the clouds change into magical shapes. I could see figures of animals, nature, and people. At night, I would watch the stars and ask myself mind-bending questions.

One day, a man approached me wearing a camera around his neck. He was so awkward with it that it looked like a prop. He was supposedly a photographer. He stopped me to say he wanted to show me photos he had taken.

There were people in the distance. So, I wasn't worried he would do anything. I also had my knife in my pocket and wouldn't hesitate to use it.

These were uncommonly large photos. I somehow knew the images had been developed by hand. The first one was a photo of me running along our roof. I could see the long blond highlights I had recently added to my hair and the look of determination on my face.

He also had photos of me playing football and baseball. When I looked up, he gave me a knowing look. My heart sank. He was communicating with his eyes.

Then, he showed me photos of my younger sister in a bathing suit. She was coming back from the pool. The look he gave me made my skin crawl. Then, I went cold. You did not mess with my family.

I backed away from him and ran home. I was scared and creeped out.

The smirk on his face spoke volumes. He was telling me that I was being observed. He was telling me not to make my sister a target.

Soon after that happened, I had my first real accident. Deanna and Mish thought locking me out of the apartment was funny. This time, they locked me out on our balcony. I decided to climb on the roof to break into our front door. I kept a piece of metal hidden nearby for just such occasions.

When I pulled myself up, I slipped, and the next thing I knew, I was hanging by my fingertips. That is when I learned that fear could cause you to lose your voice. I couldn't scream for help. I knew there wasn't much time.

I watched my fingers lose their grip. When I fell from the top, I thought I was dying. I accepted what was happening. I was proud to live on my terms.

Mr. Borja, an immigrant and mechanic who was always fixing MG's in the parking lot, happened to see me fall. He was so afraid he would cause me to lose my grip that he didn't say anything.

He saved my life that day. I was inches from hitting my head on a heavy wooden partition. He managed to push me and cushion my fall. We both ended up on the ground. I was shocked.

He said, "It makes me smile when I see you run the roof." He tiptoed his fingers across his palm in a universal sign for running. He spoke English sparingly. I smiled at him.

# Chapter 31

## AGE 13, MOM'S

A few days later, I was in our apartment alone. My mom had a rough schedule. She worked nights at a tobacco factory. She had already left for the day.

The phone rang. All the kids my age spent a lot of time on the phone. My mom once got highly irritated when I stayed on the phone all night. I curled up on the balcony in a beach lounger someone left in the utility closet and talked to my best friend all night. We picked the world apart and talked about clothes, makeup, boys, and MTV.

The ringer was very loud. When I answered the phone, no one said anything. I could hear breathing. I politely asked if someone was there. The breathing became heavier.

## SHAMAN ISIS

The caller wanted me to know it was a man. I hung up the phone.

The hair on my body was standing on end. The phone rang again, and I answered. This went on for a couple of hours. After several heavy breathing calls, the man began to say terrifying things. He said he was watching me. I yelled some colorful language and hung up again.

Later, he called again. This time, he began to speak in a frightening voice. He described our apartment in detail. He told me where I was standing in the living room. Then he precisely explained what I was wearing, even commenting on the earrings I had just put on; he liked the change.

That is when I realized he was watching me. I ran to the glass balcony door and looked out. He laughed and said he was looking at me through binoculars. I thought, "Holy shit." That made sense because the other buildings were too far away.

He explained that he had been watching me for a while. I was scared to death. I was also afraid to stay in the apartment alone.

I finally got up the nerve to run for Mr. Borja's apartment. His daughter and I were friendly. She was the other athletic girl in the neighborhood.

I wanted to be around a friendly face. I also wanted to ask what I should do. Mr. Borja's daughter and I talked about it. Perverted calls were standard in the 80s. Internet porn didn't exist to satiate lonely or sick people.

As soon as I started talking, I realized my trip was a waste of time; she couldn't help me.

I was worried. I had one man showing me photos of my personal life. At the same time, another man scared me with intimate details of my movements. The fact that they used high-tech equipment was not lost on me.

I took both as a threat. Were these the same men who had followed me throughout my childhood? Honestly, how could they not be?

I had thought about calling the police. However, I was scared. I had seen uniforms and badges on men who followed me. I had also seen how the police treated poor people.

I watched how violent some could get with folks who didn't have means.

One of our neighbors was a policeman. He knew an awful lot about our family. I always wondered why he lived there. He could easily afford to live somewhere nicer.

He kept a close eye on us. His kid and I were friendly. One day at a local store, he showed me how to steal clothes. I was shocked and deeply disappointed.

SHAMAN ISIS

After that, I intuitively knew that I should not tell him what had been going on. I had the weirdest feeling that he already knew.

I was on my own, as usual.

## Chapter 32

## AGE 13, COLLIERVILLE

A couple of weeks after moving in with Shirley and Jimmy, I snuck a call to my best friend, Tanoa. She had not heard from me since the night I told her I couldn't celebrate her birthday.

The call went differently than expected. My best friend's family answered. They said she wrapped her Firebird passenger seat-first around a pole right after I left Memphis.

Tanoa went off the road and hit one telephone pole. She was ejected from the car, hit the next pole head-on, and nearly took her head off.

I was speechless when they said doctors sewed her head to her neck. She was in critical condition. They weren't sure if she was going to make it. I asked about seeing her. They were unsure if she would ever wake up.

Later, I realized I might have died if I had stayed with my mom. I was supposed to be in that passenger seat that night.

I became angry when I learned my foster parents knew about the accident. Shirley saw my "near-death" experience as a sign that I should share my story with others. I had so many close calls with death that it was hard to disagree. Still, I was angry. I wanted to yell, are you sure you want me to share my journey with others?

I have been helping people since I was a child. I learned to use my energy and words to provide direction and help others feel better. Giving speeches to church groups seemed like a natural extension of my work. I enjoyed supporting other people.

While many people felt my childhood was terrible, I saw it as a chance to grow and learn as much as possible. That is one reason I didn't waste my time complaining.

One of the things that kept me going throughout my challenges was my spirit guides. They have been with me all my life, providing wisdom and guidance at essential moments.

One important lesson they taught me was that justice is an internal job. If going after someone bad would make life worse, get revenge by living the best life possible. They also taught me that it was wise to use every experience to grow as a person.

My new high school was pretty cool. My home life may have been weird, but my school was one of the best in Tennessee. Most of the kids were lovely. Their innocence took some time to get accustomed to.

This time in my life was the antithesis of my early school days. I was involved in activities like the arts and sports.

People got the wrong idea about my life because I rode to school limousine-style for the first couple of years.

One of my neighbors gave me a ride to school every day. He rode up front with his father. I rode in the back of their fancy car by myself, which gave people the idea that I was from a wealthy family. "No, I didn't ride to school in a limo," I would answer.

My favorite part of school was art class and volleyball practice. My advisor wanted me to become an artist. The fact that she ran the department was just a side note.

Shirley let me major in art but clarified that it had no future. At first, she let me do art because she wasn't sure I was smart enough for a "real" major. After she realized I was bored in school, she pressured me to go to college and become a teacher or preacher.

I played volleyball with some of the most incredible girls in school. Nicki McCray and Denise Lippy were terrific athletes. Nicki was a world-class volleyball and basketball player. Denise, also great at b-ball, was the best volleyball player on the team.

Denise and I became good friends. She lived around the corner from my foster parents. Denise didn't talk for the sake of talking. I liked that about her.

I knew that she was a lesbian but could have cared less. People were not out in the 80s.

My first sexual encounters were with women. I always felt it was natural. Women were a safe way to explore my sexuality. The boys had big mouths and busy hands. I understood Denise.

She gave me rides to and from volleyball practice. Which was pretty cool considering she drove a mint condition 67 Camero SS in bright cherry red. That car was amazing. She explained it was one of the benefits of her father wanting a boy. Her dad rebuilt muscle cars in his garage.

She had this great acceptance of the situation that spoke to her intelligence.

These were good days. It was the 80s, and *Top Gun* was a big hit at the box office. All the boys wore aviator glasses and leather jackets to school.

Jimmy may have made my life awkward, but school helped me blossom.

My foster parents and I spent a lot of time going to church. We were there three days a week for Sunday service, Sunday school, Bible study, and youth group. Nearly everyone in town went to church.

At least our church danced. The Baptist church did not. That meant everyone came to our church dances. These events were the highlight of being a Methodist.

Shirley could get very sanctimonious about other people's religious practices. I found her judgment grating. Is that what the church was for, creating hierarchies? I sometimes wondered if their religious beliefs weren't subconsciously out of guilt.

She spent much time training me to be a "good wife." I spent time wondering if she had mistaken me for Cinderella. She had me cleaning all the time. I had no problem showing gratitude, but this was craziness. Does the silver need to be polished every week?

I loved learning to cook. Shirley was an accomplished chef. She taught me to make everything from scratch. These were the times when we got along well. Most of the time, we were oil and water.

# Chapter 33

## AGE 14, COLLIERVILLE

Church events are a big deal in the South. I often gave speeches on making good life choices (oh, the irony!) at fairs, seminars, retreats, and fundraisers.

The church is how I met my first boyfriend; ironically, his name was Jimmy. He spotted me at a spiritual event. He approached me, and we talked for a few minutes. He was charming enough to overcome my desire to be with someone taller. His handsome features, intelligent brown eyes, talent, and drive were intriguing.

He was the first brilliant boy I met. He had just shared his own story with the church group. He was caught in Europe doing an eight-ball of cocaine and promptly kicked out of the country.

His parents had packed him off to rehab, and he had been clean for a while. He was a great speaker. I was also interested in his story and liked that he was a bad boy turned good boy.

He asked me if I was interested in him because of his car. I cut him dead on the spot. I didn't even know what kind of car he drove. Walking away, I realized he was trying to tell me he had a cool car.

I was surprised that his family contacted my foster parents to ask if he could get to know me. The fact that he was a born-again Christian and respected speaker did the trick.

My foster father clarified they would keep a close eye on my dates. He explained that getting physical was not going to happen. He added that "they" would make sure of it. He gave me the strangest look when he said that.

Jimmy, my beau, was put through the wringer. Our "dates" occurred in my foster parent's home during the first few months. Finally, we were allowed to go out on actual dates.

The fact that my boyfriend wanted to be a pilot was pretty cool. The movie *Top Gun* influenced him. He said he was considering becoming an Air Force pilot. He understood manifestation.

His red Z28 was incredible. It had nitrous oxide and was supposedly very fast; I never got to find out.

When I got home from our first actual date, my foster father told me everything we did while we were out. I wanted to smack the grin off his face.

How did he know all the details of our date? He reminded me that getting intimate would not end well.

After that, I paid closer attention. I finally understood why I was being allowed to date. It is because men were spying on my dates.

That realization made me feel very awkward on dates. There were times when I could feel eyes on us. I would search out the energy and find a man with binoculars or a camera. They always dressed well and drove nice cars.

Once, my boyfriend Jimmy and I went to the park to make out. I could feel that we were being watched. I wanted to learn all about intimacy. I did not want to do it while someone was watching.

My boyfriend and I were getting comfortable on the blanket when a man appeared beside us wearing binoculars. He stood a few feet away. I could tell that he was there to stop us from making out. My face turned bright red. I was so embarrassed.

After the man finally left, I tried to explain how weird it was to my boyfriend. He was so irritated at being interrupted he couldn't see what I was trying to point out.

When I asked him what he thought of the man standing there until we got up to leave, he called him a pervert. My intuition told me not to bother explaining that men were following us.

How would he understand if he couldn't see how weird this man was acting? I was also humiliated by the whole bizarre situation.

I didn't want my boyfriend to think it was a reflection of me. In the 80s, society often blamed female victims. One day, I would be glad I hadn't bothered to tell him.

Jimmy, my foster father, took great pleasure in telling me the details of all my dates. He was thrilled to know everything I did.

Over time, I saw the same group of men on rotation. They included a man in a police uniform.

I met several kind police officers in Collierville. I knew that police officers were not all bad. Every profession has a few bad people.

# Chapter 34

## AGE 26, NYC

Today was a busy day. I had several appointments at the boutique. I loved my job with Robert Marc. His attention to detail and customer service was unparalleled. He taught me how to give someone an unforgettable styling experience. His training is one of the reasons my clients included such interesting people.

Financiers Thomas Lee and Christopher Burch were popping by for an eyewear fitting. They were always kind and full of fascinating stories.

Thomas worked right next door. He was making waves in the finance world and had even bought Snapple.

Christopher always wore funny little Dutch slippers. At first, I didn't know what to make of him. Then, I realized he chose humor and comfort over trends. Speaking with such dynamic people taught me a great deal about the world.

Nowadays, my name, Cynthia Lucci, isn't the only thing that has changed. My life is so much different. I look like a completely new person. My accent is tamed, and my style is more polished.

I splurged on a great hair stylist and learned to wear clothing that elegantly showcased my figure.

My face thinned out. My older sister even asked me if I had gotten facial surgery. I found it insulting but comforting.

In retrospect, the distinctive shag haircut for the Paul Mitchell campaign was nearly identical to the haircut I had when I moved in with my foster parents. I also didn't wear much makeup in the national ad, making me look a lot like I did in high school. Since then, I have avoided making the same mistake.

Having a long-term boyfriend in the city made me feel much safer. Not that I was going to tell him my real story. He tended to share every detail of anything I did tell him, so I told him almost nothing.

At this point, I didn't want my carefully crafted life messed up by old news and stalkers. I was aware that I wasn't just hiding in plain sight. I was hiding from my past.

I still did some modeling for extra money. Not looking or sounding like "Cindy" anymore was an asset.

These days, hiding is easier.

I booked *The Conan O'Brien Show* again. I was not worried about being spotted on a show like O'Brien's. Shirley and Jimmy did not watch late-night TV. Their religious crew didn't watch shows with naughty humor. I doubted anyone would ever recognize me anymore. I looked completely different as an adult.

*The Conan O'Brien Show* has already booked me as an actress for several segments. I got to slap one actor for pretending to get fresh with me at the Museum of Modern Art. I remember we were standing in front of an Edward Hopper painting. I thought it was funny that he wanted me to slap him hard.

His request did give me pause. Several friends told me that I would make a great dominatrix. I was never sure how to take that comment. I went full-on with the slap. You can hear it on the tape. He was a method actor, after all.

I did one segment on the beach. It was a great way to see the Hamptons.

My favorite segment on Conan's show was where I wore a nurse's uniform and sang Happy Birthday. I spent time with the cast. Every time I was on, I met the people appearing that evening.

MEMORY MANSION

My mom got a kick out of my stories. She was the most animated when I told her about famous people. She was fascinated but no longer surprised by my life's turn.

# Chapter 35

## AGE 26, NYC

My friends and I had just rollerbladed the length of the city. We were hungry and decided to go to Bubba's restaurant for breakfast. The couple I was hanging out with was a lot of fun. They had a healthy relationship and enjoyed being active together.

My beeper went off. So, I went outside the downtown hotspot to use the pay phone. While dialing, I looked up to find the actor Harvey Keitel looking at me. He was in the movie we had a poster of in San Diego, *Pulp Fiction*.

He told me that I had an interesting look. He heard my twang in the restaurant. He asked about my accent. When I told him I was from Memphis, he nodded. He mentioned he was doing a movie about Elvis.

He asked me to come to his production company. I could tell it was professional and not personal.

So, I went by a few days later. Harvey complimented my motorcycle jacket. It was beige with black stripes down the arms. I recently got my motorcycle license and a Harley Davidson 1200 in turquoise and cream. I loved riding bikes because it reminded me of free-running and rooftops.

Harvey and I talked about Memphis. I did not mention meeting Elvis when I was young. Being secretive was a blessing and a curse. It sounded like bragging to my ears. So, I never told anyone.

He wanted to hear original accents from the South. The next time we met, I called my mother from his apartment. Honestly, it was not much help.

Here was another chance to promote my acting; something similar happened with Harold Ramis, and I held back again.

I recently landed an acting agent at Abrams Artists but wondered if I should bother.

Harvey's assistant was puttering around his apartment. She asked me interesting questions. Later, we walked out together.

She asked me about my life and dreams as we walked to the subway. After a bit, she told me that she thought acting was great but would not satisfy me like the business world. She told me that my head was the most exciting thing about me. That made me smile.

She told me that listening to how I thought about the world made her feel I should focus on my career. She added that I could change how people think about things.

On my way home, I knew the whole reason I had met Harvey Keitel was so that I could have this conversation. It rang with how I was already feeling. I had been dancing around acting for years. It just didn't interest me enough.

I wanted to be a respected businesswoman, not an actress. It was tempting, but my work at Robert Marc had shown me what sitting across from influential business people was like. That seemed far more appealing than how women were treated in the acting world in the 90s, especially women from the modeling industry.

PR is going to be the next big thing. The way mass media was unfolding in my mid-20s, I knew it would be compelling. I wanted to learn how to influence culture and media.

After that meeting with Harvey and his assistant, I decided to focus on PR. I was already handling a lot of the media and interviews for Robert.

I just knew it was the right move.

## Chapter 36

## AGE 26, NYC

I still had auditions. Who turned away the extra money? Occasionally, I would get delayed at auditions and get in trouble at work. I was one of the top salespeople and popular with VIPs. That gave me some breathing room.

Once, I was stuck on my way to an audition for what seemed like hours. The taxi driver just kept apologizing. He didn't know what the hold-up was; I regretted taking the audition.

When I got to the point of climbing the taxi walls, I would get rocked out of my impatience by the most bizarre sight. Crossing the road right in front of us were three elephants. There was a monkey on each elephant's back. It was bizarre. The universe was speaking to me, trying to tell me I had a monkey on my back, but I had stopped listening.

When I first saw the elephants, I wondered if the stress of the audition was getting to me. The crazy sight made us both start laughing.

I always tried to find humor in stressful situations. I also made it a point to be kind to anyone I met. I was on the receiving end of the hierarchy system. I never wanted to treat anyone that way.

When I returned to the boutique, my boss and friend Jamie rang my bell. He asked me what on earth had happened. When Jamie saw my face, he lost the sarcasm. When I told him what happened, he laughed and said, "That must mean the circus is in town." I had a front-row seat to the big guys crossing the city.

The next day, I decided to go by Gucci. I had been eyeballing a bamboo handle bag. I learned to splurge on good shoes and purses. A woman can look like a million bucks in basics if her shoes and handbag are refined.

Logos were becoming a big deal in fashion. I have visited this particular handbag several times. It was embossed black on black with G's, so pretty. This time, I was going to buy it. I paid part in cash and the rest on a card. The bag was worth every penny.

It was great timing as I had an appointment with a New York Times writer named Rene. He was going to help me put that bag to use eventually. He didn't know it yet.

Robert sent me media and VIPs. They were a mix of big-name news personalities, musicians, actors selecting eyewear for TV and film roles, and VIPs photographed at events—special needs called for special treatment.

Working with the VIPs would lead to me styling a lot of iconic film and TV characters. The projects I worked on were cool.

I did eyewear for the leads in *The Sopranos* for their first season. Lorraine Bracco and James Gandolfini were very kind. Sunglasses and eyeglasses were often a critical part of a character's look and style and ended up in posters and ad campaigns. That was true for *The Sopranos*.

Eyewear is essential in acting because it frames the face, requires the viewer to look through the lens, and speaks to the character's style and personality. Talented actors take eyewear seriously.

I also handled a lot of TV interviews. I was careful to stick to TV shows and news that the folks back home didn't watch, like MTV's *House of Style*.

In the 90s, the media was very regionalized. So, I wasn't that worried. I wanted to keep my background private.

That kind of thing would get in the way of the career I wanted. PR and "scandalous" life stories did not mix.

    I heard it was common for top PR people to sign legal documents about what they could and could not do while working for a big-name brand. It made me more determined not to let my history or the bad guys catch up.

# Chapter 37

## AGE 6, THE ORPHANAGE

One day, my father unexpectedly arrived at Saint Peter's. I was impressed that he got past the nuns and irritated to see him get special treatment.

Sister Anne Elizabeth came to tell me he wanted to see me. She sent me beautiful energy to prepare me for the unexpected visit.

I was Dean's "favorite." Honestly, it was because we looked so much alike. It used to worry me that looking like my father was a life sentence.

We met by the tire swing. I climbed in and started swaying as my father approached. His beautiful brown eyes were clear, and he wasn't high.

I knew my mother had no idea he was in town. I was not going to tell her. She never bad-mouthed my father, but I knew she was upset about what happened.

He knelt beside me and discussed how he screwed everything up for the family. I did an internal eye roll. I was not quick to believe adults. My memories of him were not dreamy childhood tales. I didn't hate him. I thought of him as weak.

He said that he had stopped drinking. I took this to mean he stopped taking drugs as well. I was glad to see him looking better.

I remember the visit made me sad. Not because my father had come to visit but because of what I realized about my dad's future.

I often knew the truth about people. It is hard to explain unless you are "gifted" with intuition at a young age. I knew that he would not live to see me as an adult. It softened my attitude.

I understood I was seeing him as he should have lived, proud and healthy.

He took a coin out of his pocket and handed it to me. He was very proud of it. I remember seeing the word change on the coin. It stood out to me as I knew it to be one of the most consistent things in life.

The saying on the coin stuck in my mind. It read, "God, grant me the serenity to accept the things I cannot change, the courage to change the things I can, and the wisdom to know the difference."

It was a special moment that would be the most important we would ever have together.

The lesson in that prayer defined many of the decisions I would make in my future.

I was sad he would not live to see old age.

# Chapter 38

## AGE 9, THE ORPHANAGE

The local teachers were on strike. It was so weird to see them standing outside the school holding signs. There was a crackle of defiance in the air. The principal seemed worried.

My circumstances gave me an odd freedom at school. I didn't get in much trouble when I was busted for climbing the building and running around the roof. It was well-known that I was a bit of a wild child.

I remember being irritated when I went from learning from the sisters to attending school. I wanted to write with my left hand. I tried to switch from right to left again. Which was akin to saying you wanted to worship Satan.

Adults told me that no one would be able to take me seriously. They implied that people who wrote with their left hand had mental health issues and less chance of success. I thought this was absurd. At one point, I let my mask drop and responded, "Even animals use everything they've got!"

They assumed my remark had something to do with my "issues." I noticed some adults thought I had learning problems. Nope, I was bored out of my mind. That is why I skipped a lot of classes.

That is not to say I didn't get along with many teachers; I did. That was about to be useful for one of my more unusual childhood memories.

The teachers had been on strike for long enough to make administrators nervous. I remember people saying do not cross the line. As if it was a major national strike, it was local. So, I thought nothing of chatting briefly with them on my way in.

Whenever the principal saw me speak to the teachers, he asked me what they said. Then, the teachers would ask me what he said.

All the students were hanging out in the cafeteria because the admins thought closing the school would cause the strike to drag on. Parents also needed the school to remain open. These are the reasons we were given class in mass in the cafeteria.

SHAMAN ISIS

I remember the day well. The concept of time was messing with my head. I was paying attention to how fast or slow it went by; it didn't make sense. I had already noticed that time sped up with age. I kept closing my eyes and trying to control the speed of it using the wall clock.

When I opened my eyes again, I saw one of the teachers hiding near the back stairwell. She was trying to get my attention.

The teachers were a mix of black and white women. They wanted improved pay and benefits. I had a lot of sympathy because of what I saw my mother go through.

The teacher laid her finger across her lips in a universal sign of secrecy. Like most buildings, I knew every inch of the school.

A few minutes later, I surprised her by popping up behind her. She gave me a funny look of approval. Then, she nodded and said, "That is what they are talking about."

We snuck to the parking lot, where two other teachers were waiting. I was fascinated by this turn of events.

They said they needed my help. There were papers in the principal's office, and they needed to know what they said. They told me that if they could find out what the records said, they could end the strike. They wanted to return to their jobs only after getting what they deserved.

That is when they made my mouth drop open. They knew my size and stealth meant I could get in and out of the building unseen. They asked me if I could safely get into the principal's office to bring them a folder about the strike.

I was thrilled. I said yes. These women needed my help. If I timed it right, I could do what they asked me to do.

I waited until the next day. I chatted with the teachers on my way in and told them when I would do it.

While the administrators, including the principal, were in the cafeteria taking the role, I was sneaking into his inner sanctum. I felt like a spy, a real-life spy.

I quietly dropped into his office. I walked over to his papers and went through them until I found the folder for the strike. I got scared a few times when I heard someone outside his office. My little heart was racing.

As asked, I took the whole folder. Initially, I thought about figuring out what the ladies were looking for, but I needed help understanding. I remember it concerned what they were willing to offer the teachers.

The ladies looked relieved when I met them in the parking lot. One kept mumbling about how terrible it was that they were using a kid. The other two just said shush.

They looked very excited when they read one page in particular. They chattered. Finally, they straightened the folder and handed it back.

They asked me if I was sure I was okay taking it back. Whatever they had read was helpful. I knew I would be okay.

I climbed the building and dropped into his office. I put the folder back with a smile on my face. I was walking on air. The strike ended a few days later, and the teachers were happy.

It was my little secret. I wouldn't tell anyone about what happened for some 40 years.

Some secrets are fun to keep.

# Chapter 39

## AGE 13, MOM'S

My best friend Tanoa and I were going to meet some friends heading to Shelby Farms. We called it the beach. It was a big lake that everyone treated like a beach.

My mom would sleep most of the day. She would never know. I threw an Oxford dress shirt over my bathing suit. I had no idea where the shirt came from, but it made the perfect swim cover. My boobs had popped recently. I was not happy about the change.

Being tall made doing backflips challenging enough. Now, I had these puppies to contend with; I was not amused. The boys were starting to treat me differently. I preferred being one of the guys.

I told my sisters I would read, lay out, and go by the pool. I pulled myself up on the roof. I went to the other end of the building and climbed back down. I could count on no one looking for me for a few hours.

I walked over to the Tompson's place. They lived in a house next to the school. Their dad had passed away and left behind a widow who eased her pain with pills. I had noticed that if drugs came in bottles from the pharmacy, everyone nodded in understanding.

Many mothers took over-the-counter dexedrine to stay thin and calmed themselves with pills from the pharmaceutical world. The pill industry had me worried about the future. Really, how was this different from illegal drugs and alcohol?

Anyway, this made her one of the "cool moms."

Tanoa met me at their house. Eight of us piled into Ms. Tompson's station wagon. We drove for a while. Shelby Farms was just outside of Memphis.

Finally, we stopped at a service station close to the lake. The adults bought lots of beer, ice, and cigarettes. On the drive, I noticed Ms. Tompson's new beau was aggressive. By the time we left the gas station, I knew he must have begun drinking before we left the house. His energy gave me a strange feeling.

I was going to lie down in the back of the station wagon but decided to hop in the front to keep an eye on him. He was making me nervous. As we were leaving the gas station, I had a bad feeling. I said something about being careful about the heavy traffic and cops.

He pulled out. We crossed the big highway to make a left. I looked over my shoulder and saw an 18-wheeler crossing the intersection behind us. I knew; I just knew something terrible was about to happen.

I warned him that we were in serious trouble. For some reason, he decided to keep turning into the lane. He had this look on his face like he would prove the world wrong. I watched as this massive truck and station wagon headed for each other.

The truck was so big that the station wagon got dragged under it. I heard metal crushing and glass shattering. I looked up to see the roof buckling over my head. It felt like a giant can opener was taking the top off.

Our car was no match for the underside of a gigantic truck. Suddenly, I knew both vehicles' tires would collide and cause a severe accident. I slid further into the floorboard, dragging Tanoa with me. The roof was caving in, and glass was flying around the wagon. I felt the tires of both vehicles collide, and suddenly, our car shot into the sky.

The car flipped once and flew so high into the air that it crossed back over the medium we passed on the turn. I could not believe how fast we were going. We flipped two more times before coming to a rest upside down. I counted the number of times I saw grass and sky.

I do not know how I got out. I found myself standing on the side of the road with glass embedded all over my skin. My hands and feet were dripping blood, and dozens of small pieces of glass were sticking out of my body.

I remember helping some of the passengers. I helped some climb out, pulled broken glass out of bleeding skin, and comforted those stuck in the vehicle.

The trunk of the station wagon was obliterated.

I stood there staring at the wreck when a local newspaper took a photograph. I had come close to dying again.

Eventually, I would realize that the accident gave Deanna enough truth to get me sent to juvie. The details she fabricated tipped my fate over the edge. The scandal also got the attention of my foster parents.

My mom cried when she saw the station wagon. It made me feel terrible. I wanted to scream that I knew what I was doing, but did I?

I had already talked with Tanoa about wanting to be successful someday. I added that I would take school seriously and stop skipping class.

## Chapter 40

## AGE 8, THE ORPHANAGE

I visited some fascinating foster families when I was young. Sometimes, we went on trips where I was often in the company of their only child.

I remember a Winnebago trip to a national forest. On the way there, the mom served peanut butter, mayonnaise, and banana sandwiches, which I promptly tucked in the trash.

There was one wealthy family who lived in a modern-day palace. Their daughter and I would go to the kitchen in the middle of the night to eat ice cream from one of their freezers. They had a fridge filled with giant ice cream barrels. It was awesome.

Once, I went to Disneyland with another family. I remember getting dizzy and vomiting after one ride, then promptly hopping on a roller coaster. I have always loved roller coasters.

My favorite trip was to Alabama. We went on an extended vacation. I tasted space ice cream and hung out with people who worked for NASA. I got a behind-the-scenes tour. I have fond memories of that trip. The scientists and engineers from NASA were the first adults to treat me like I had a brain in my head.

While at a picnic with these great minds, I started taking toys apart. I liked figuring out what made them work. Instead of getting upset with me like the sisters, they encouraged me to dismantle and reassemble the toys.

I was so excited not to get in trouble that I opened my mouth, dropped my mask, and started asking questions. They laughed when they realized I was curious about all sorts of things.

Imagine my surprise when I would get to work with the folks at NASA decades later.

One vacation also sticks out; I was with Shirley and Jimmy. We were at an amusement park. The 70s were fun because kids got to do things that would not fly in the future.

We trailed from ride to ride, stopping for food at one point. Lines were always a thing at parks. Jimmy and I stood in line the longest for the newest ride in the park. It was a giant circle. A U-shaped bar dropped over your head, so your legs dangled like a ski lift.

We waited for our turn. Many people were chickening out—the idea of being upside down with only a metal harness to hold you in scared them away.

When it was our turn, we eagerly climbed up. The operator lowered the metal bar onto our chests. The ride started spinning. People were laughing and yelling colorful words. The world was flying by fast.

Suddenly, my harness opened up completely. I felt myself falling out. I was upside down and no longer being held by anything. I was freakishly calm. Jimmy's arm snapped out, and he grabbed a fistful of my shirt and shorts. The look on his face was terrifying.

We spun a couple more times, with me hanging by his grip. I am sure I passed out at that point.

When I could focus, I saw they were closing the ride. The operator was sheet white. People did not want to get on it anymore.

I remember thinking that Jimmy was meant to save me that day. No one had a grip as he did. It came from years of fixing cars and changing tires. He was shaking and angry.

## SHAMAN ISIS

No one understood how my harness came open. About a half hour later, I was ready for the next ride.

My rebound game was strong.

# Chapter 49

## AGE 32, NYC

I loved working with Restaurant Associates, which manages iconic NYC landmark food and beverage spaces. The executives appreciated my guidance. I enjoyed working with all of them.

After the success of Brasserie 8 1/2, they asked me to consult on public relations and marketing for their portfolio. That was an enormous compliment. Nadine was pleased. I was happy because I knew I could open an agency of my own soon.

I was finally getting the respect I had been striving for my whole career.

Restaurant Associates handled America's most famous buildings, including Rockefeller Center, Lincoln Center, and the World Trade Center. I was honored and shocked at my list of new clients. I already have famed hotelier Ian Schrager, restaurateur Jeffrey Chodorow, and billionaire Sheldon Solow on my client list. I wasn't sure it would get better.

My mother couldn't believe it. She thought I might become an actress. She may have confused my decades of masking with a love of acting.

I have been mirroring acceptable behavior for as long as I can remember. I had cached so many personalities and behaviors I had become a chameleon. I fit in everywhere I went.

A businesswoman that no one knew anything about, not really: I was forever being told by people how mysterious I was. My history was a mystery.

Honestly, I just wanted respect and results. This outcome was the best of both worlds.

When I first moved to New York, I spent years commuting through the World Trade Center. Now, I can work with the incredible team running the restaurant at the top. They wanted me to make it hotter than 8 1/2, which was a lot because 8 1/2 was booked months out.

All of these landmarks were engineering and design marvels. The architects, chefs, and artisans involved in these projects were world-class. I adored working with all the remarkably talented people.

I got to know foodies like William Grimes and Florence Fabricant. William and I even got into a PR battle that started a national conversation about comfort food. CNN's Jeannie Moos did a national segment on the debate. Should or shouldn't restaurants serve mom-style cooking? It was a lot of fun. Jeannie is a hoot.

I was knee-deep in strategy meetings. I finally had a plan for Windows on the World. I would make it a go-to for the finance, arts, and entertainment crowd. I have been reaching out to media, event producers, and entertainment people to book some incredible opportunities for the space.

I was thrilled to highlight the work of industry icons Michael Lomonaco, David Emil, and Joe Baum. They were famous in the restaurant world. I was obsessed with getting them more accolades.

# Chapter 42

## AGE 30, NYC

It was the morning of September 11th. My husband Dave, whom I married the year before, drove us downtown. I was supposed to go by the World Trade Center for a meeting. For some reason, I didn't go to Windows on the World that day. Intuition whispers; it doesn't yell.

I expect to be at the World Trade Center a lot in the coming months. I wanted to make sure the work I did was perfect. The buildings held a special place in my heart because they had survived a vicious attack in the early 90s, and I felt a kinship with the iconic location. The Twin Towers were a symbol of enduring freedom.

We were driving downtown. The last thing I expected to see was a plane running into the World Trade Center. I thought I might be seeing things, but the smoke made it clear that I was not hallucinating.

I couldn't catch my breath or my thoughts. I knew that evil had arrived on a scale so epic it would shock the world. I knew immediately that this was a purposeful act.

I had to get out of the car. I was going to throw up. I knew a lot of people were going to die. I couldn't even speak. I was so terrified. My skin started burning, and I began to get awful visions about what would happen.

I had to get to the office. I needed to warn people. First, I had to throw up. So, I bent over and let go of my breakfast. The things I could see in my visions were making me violently ill. I felt like I was back at Saint Peter's, incapable of helping some of the children when the men came in the night.

My husband, a cancer drug rep, headed to a hospital downtown. I ran to my office on 18th Street, two miles from the World Trade Center.

When I arrived, I was surprised my coworkers were at their computers. They were behaving like it was any other day of the week. I tried calling Windows on the World and the World Trade Center but grew frustrated.

I turned on the TV next to my desk but got irritated that no one in the office was paying attention. I tried explaining what I saw in my visions, but people kept working on their computers. I tried calling the authorities and the restaurant. Finally, I went downstairs.

I turned on Nadine and Richard's second-floor TV. I just wanted to confirm what was happening. My visions were vivid; both buildings would collapse.

I watched the second plane hit. It felt like the blood had left my body. I was white with shock.

Then, I started pacing the townhouse and yelling louder at my coworkers.

I ran outside and tried speaking to anyone in uniform, and they looked more overwhelmed than I did.

In my mind's eye, I could see what would happen to both towers. I saw fuel running down the elevator shaft. The fire would get so hot that it would weaken the buildings. I tried explaining what was going to happen to my coworkers and uniforms. I realized that I sounded hysterical.

Some people told me that what I saw would not happen, that a collapse was scientifically impossible. I intuitively knew that wasn't true.

My visions had never been wrong before. I never shared them with others because I feared how I would be treated.

However, I had counted on them to keep me safe for years. I asked anyone I could get a hold of to get people out. It was too late for most people on the upper floors, especially the restaurant.

I remember feeling the victims' relief when they thought they would get rescued. When they accepted what was happening, the praying, crying, and begging reached heartbreaking levels.

I thought I would go insane hearing so many people give up. I turned my intuition off when they started jumping off the building. I had to stop hearing their thoughts and feelings.

I tried to tell people to cover their faces because the air was poisonous. Nadine and I got into an argument about it. No one wanted to believe it was toxic.

The people I worked with were in survival mode. I, on the other hand, was so accustomed to trauma that I didn't realize I was the one acting unusually.

At some point, my phone stopped working. Earlier, I made a decision not to call my mother. I didn't want her to hear how upset I was; I couldn't tell her what I saw happening. She would have freaked out; it was too much to burden her.

I was thinking of how to get off the island but knew it was too late. The city was getting locked down, and people were in shock everywhere. They wandered the streets covered in ash and cried out for missing loved ones.

I helped. Some people just needed a hug or to scream or cry. Finally, the air became so bad I had to get away. I knew we would lose thousands of people in the years to come because of the smoke.

I became incandescent when the EPA got on national television and told people the atmosphere was not toxic. They should have known the truth. I wondered if they had a choice.

In the following days, I tried to talk to people about the air. They wanted to believe what talking heads were saying.

Afterward, I sunk into a depression but thought I was okay. I wasn't. I moved out of the city not long after that. I never spoke about what happened to anyone.

I needed to talk to someone about how I felt. I should have been able to do more. Even though I knew intellectually, it was too late.

Until then, my husband's nickname for me was the fun police. I was very safety conscious and liked to be in control. That was about to change. My drinking was about to start climbing.

# Chapter 43

## AGE 12, MOM'S

I dreamed of jumping rope in a frilly pink outfit and roller skates. When I had the dream a third time, I wrote it in my diary, which I kept on the roof of the building. I was not taking any chances since I regularly read my sister's diary.

Soon after, the church gave me a box of used goods. I was delighted to find roller skates in the box. I threw on one of the outfits and set off to skate. I was a natural.

One of my most heartbreaking childhood experiences was being naturally athletic and unable to take lessons in any sports I was good at, like ice skating and gymnastics. So, I added roller skating to the sports I taught myself. I was doing axles before the day was out.

On my first cruise through the apartment complex, a girl approached me. We started talking. She was a young black girl about my age. She asked me if I wanted to play with her and her sister. I said yes. We went to her apartment. I started getting the oddest feeling.

Her sister came out of their apartment holding a jump rope. They dared me to jump in my skates. The whole time this was happening, I was getting hot and tingly. I began jumping rope. I realized I was wearing a frilly pink twin-set from the donation box—a frilly pink outfit precisely like the one in my dream.

I stopped jumping and sat down. It had been a while since I had prophetic visions. The last one was while I was in care the year before. It brought back a lot of memories of Saint Peter's. I excused myself and raced home.

I went to my rooftop and read the diary entry. I kept some personal items wrapped in a container and hidden in an old breaker box, which included my diary.

I described everything that happened, even the flowers and ruffles on my outfit. The whole thing was messing with my head. I was hoping that what happened growing up was a fluke.

I talked to my spirit guides about it. They pointed out how often the visions had saved me from serious harm. That is when I began to accept that my visions were a secret gift. I wasn't about to tell anyone or get sent to an insane asylum.

I knew I needed to make it up with my new friends. I had taken off suddenly.

The sisters, Joy and Janice, were about my age and friendly. I went by and asked them to come outside. I told Joy about what happened in my dreams. I don't know why I told her, but I knew she would understand.

She said it sounded like deja vu. Her mom got deja vu a lot. I had to look that phrase up when I got the chance. It wasn't quite the same as what was happening with my dreams, but I had experienced it many times. It always made the hair on my body stand on end.

Joy, Janice, and I had an easy understanding. All of us had difficult childhoods. So, we decided that we would have fun together.

We learned about hail when saucer-sized ice balls dented cars in the parking lot in front of their apartment. We stood under an awning with our mouths hanging open. It was epic.

We loved dancing together. We would bring the boom box out and sing to all the hits. When Michael Jackson's song Thriller came out, we played it repeatedly.

## SHAMAN ISIS

One day, I asked them to teach me how to dance. They said I was a pretty good dancer. I explained that I didn't want to dance like a white person, which made them howl.

They loved my request. Joy responded, "The problem with white people is they worry too much about what other people think about how they look."

I hugged her because it was the truth.

# Chapter 44

## AGE 13, MOM'S

Babysitting was the best way to make money. So, as soon as I could, I started watching local kids. Babysitting is how I found out how many people smoked pot. I did not think marijuana was any worse than alcohol.

At the time, marijuana was demonized in a way that seemed over the top, a screaming red flag. I assumed this was due to a big industry paying the right people; I was not wrong.

How else would alcohol and prescription drugs corner the market if people could grow their remedies? I said that I hoped it would be legal by 2000. I didn't know anyone who got beaten by a stoned parent. I knew plenty that got hit by a drunk one.

I didn't think the American people would let themselves be led around by the nose for more than twenty more years.

So, this was my excuse to try pot. My sister and friends had already introduced me to cigarettes, Boone's Farm, and Budweiser. The first time I smoked pot, I ate myself sick. They told me that it was called the munchies.

At school, we had a thing called Goat Hill. It was a grassy hill between the middle and high schools. That was where the kids who smoked would go to puff away. The occasional rebel would light up a joint. It was far enough that teachers had a hard time catching the culprit.

Older teens could legally smoke cigarettes in those days. That will change soon.

They were working on a law to make the drinking age 21. Some people felt that if you could send your son to war at 18, making the minimum drinking age 21 was absurd. I figured they would make some exceptions for young military men.

As much as I got into a shit ton of trouble in those days, I liked to be in control of myself. Pot made me overthink. The mind is a dangerous place!

Pills were becoming more and more common. I got to sample quaaludes before they were yanked from the market. It's funny how being pill-shaped prevented prescription drugs from being labeled as hard.

I would not touch cocaine, heroin, morphine, or syringes. They scared me because they reminded me of my father.

I sold small amounts of pot to friends. I was by no means a dealer. It had more to do with removing my stash before it spoiled.

Not long before the crap hit the fan, I tried acid. It was blotter acid. At first, it was too much. I couldn't even see.

Once I took my very high self to my room, I had an all-night existential conversation about the meaning of life. I went through my memory mansion and made decisions about my life's direction.

After that, I told my best friend I wanted to take my future seriously. I wanted to learn.

That acid trip at age 12 sent me back down the spiritual path. I have always been spiritually inclined. After that experience, I started looking into shamanism, the religion of nature, and mysticism.

I knew enough to keep it to myself! I remembered what happened when Deanna got her hands on books about witchcraft. People freaked out.

I read them but felt many were purposely bent towards occultism to make them more popular.

## SHAMAN ISIS

A few months before I moved out of my family's house, a woman I believe was a shaman or witch moved into an apartment next door. She would teach me a lot about energy.

She was a striking black woman with waist-length braids. She was exotic and fascinating. She made and sold all-natural snacks. It would be years before I would see snacks like hers in stores.

We got along instantly. The woman taught me about herbs, plants, and natural foods. She also showed me what a spiritual life could be like without religion.

I believe she was also an oracle. I would make that connection by watching *The Matrix*. I watched the movie with my friend Jamie, his best friend, and the photographer Herb Ritts. Herb didn't like the film. Which I thought was strange.

My spiritual neighbor reminded me of the prophet in the movie. The way she spoke to me about the world and life was similar.

## Chapter 45

## AGE 29, NYC

Riding motorcycles was a part of my life. I had been riding for a couple of years. We went to rallies, festivals, veterans runs, and on long trips around the country. Sturgis was my favorite event: half a million or more bikers in one tiny town. It was wild but fabulous.

I felt very at home on a motorcycle. It reminded me of free-running. I tricked out my first Harley with chrome, braids, tassels, and loud pipes. Most motorcyclists get noisy pipes to alert other drivers to their presence. Only idiots get obnoxious pipes to startle people.

I rode with a large group of guys. My sister-in-law joined occasionally. We had gotten our licenses together. I warned the group that I would not be pleased if they rode like idiots. It endangered the whole group. Something about my energy warned people not to test me on safety.

Young girls would cheer me on. Seeing a woman on a motorcycle made them smile from ear to ear. I smiled back. Somewhere, there is an epic photo of me putting on Mac lip gloss while going ninety miles an hour on a straightaway. There were no cars as far as I could see.

Guys had recently started wearing shirts that said, "If you can read this, the bitch fell off." So, I got a sticker with the saying, "If you can read this, the prick fell off," for the back of my helmet. It gave me a laugh.

Our group rode all over the country together. So, riding in NYC was something I was comfortable doing. Going through Times Square late at night is incredible.

I was about to switch from working for Robert Marc to working at a PR agency. I had taken a few days off. We were riding back to the city. As usual, the traffic leaving the George Washington Bridge was slow-moving.

I was entering the Henry Hudson Parkway when a flashy Porsche pushed closer and closer to my bike. His bumper was next to my foot. I held my lane and gave him several warnings. Finally, he hit my foot peg with his front bumper. One thing I have is a temper. If you endanger someone's life, I am going to get pissed.

I lifted my heavily booted foot high in the air and brought it down on the hood of his car. I was angry that he was oblivious to my safety. He got out to yell at me. When he saw the look on my face, he got right back in his car.

Drivers in NY are crazy. The only way to survive is to become crazier.

We were coming up to the 96th Street exit. I saw a car cutting from the inside left lane to the exit ramp. He was flying and about to put his vehicle between our two bikes. I noticed that he was ancient.

It happened quickly. I had seen enough crashes to know I did not want to hit my head on the back of his car. I hit the brakes so fast that I caused my motorcycle and myself to flip over anyway. I flew through the air, landed hard, and slid quite a ways.

I knew I had hurt my teeth, hips, back, and extremities. I was only wearing a tank top and beanie helmet; it was so stupid.

At the hospital, I surveyed the damage. I had a solid case of road rash, a fractured hip that took years to diagnose, and two fractured front teeth. I was fortunate my helmet slid in front of my face. I had deep cuts inside my lip from cushioning the blow. To this day, I have the imprint of the handlebars on my hips.

SHAMAN ISIS

When I saw the hairline fractures, I knew my two front teeth would be a problem one day. It was a prophetic moment because I knew that when they became a problem, I would be in a painful place in life.

# Chapter 46

## AGE 31, NYC

I loved working in PR. I was 31 and living it up in New York City. Cocaine is making a comeback. I worked a grueling schedule. Nadine expects us to be at our desks early, especially the morning after a big event.

We did PR for the hottest bars, nightclubs, and parties. That meant long days and nights. I often worked from eight a.m. until three a.m. or later. While good at my job, I was never comfortable socializing.

My husband was very social; it was a priority in his life. We met on a shoot, and he poured on the extrovert charm. I masked and became fantastic at acting, especially when I broke down and dabbled in cocaine.

Vodka martinis with bumps of cocaine became my fuel. As long as I was doing world-class work, I was okay, right?

The VIP scene in the early 2000s was wild. You get special treatment when you control the velvet rope at extraordinary events. That meant I was constantly surrounded by or offered the best alcohol and drugs.

My husband loved the parties. He also loved how thin and social I became when I felt good. He had teased me for years about being the fun police. Now, he thought I had the most fabulous job on the planet.

I made sure I kept my alcohol and drug use quiet. I was not about to give people ammunition to ruin my success. I kept my habits to myself.

We produced and publicized the most talked-about events. I remember the 35th anniversary of the fashion house Emanual Ungaro. It was over the top. It took place at the armory.

Models in skin-colored clothing lounged in pools of water. The buffet was outrageous.

Nadine's client list was top dog. Amy Sacco's Bungalow 8 and Jonathon Moore's Bernard were the most exclusive clubs in New York. Chateau Marmont and Standard Downtown were our top LA hangouts. Her client list brought a slew of celebrity events to the agency.

Jonathan Moore is one of my favorite clients. He has the best sushi restaurant in New York, named Bond Street. When I learned the chef served poisonous fish, I got the newspaper to do a big spread on blowfish preparation. Not even Google's new search engine had a story on blowfish.

The top chefs in the city liked to go by Jonathon's place, Bernard, after work. So I brought the *New York Post* one night, and we did a big story with Jean Georges, Daniel Boulud, Rocco DeSpirito, and other chefs hanging out together.

I remember being at Amy Sacco's Lot 61 on September 10, 2001. She introduced me to Bruce Willis. She was fabulous as the hostess du jour and always very kind to me.

I was happy to hear Bruce Willis donated so much money to the 9/11 recovery effort.

After the tragedy, I started drinking when I wasn't out for work. I would pour a martini or three to loosen up.

Eventually, I took a break from the blow. It was becoming a problem. I liked the effects too much.

# Chapter 47

## AGE 12, MOM'S

Libraries are one of my favorite places to visit. I fell in love with books as a child. They were my friend, teacher, and companion.

Skipping classes may have been my go-to, but so was spending time in the library. I always checked out the maximum number of books. I have held a library card most of my life.

My mother and foster mother were both big readers. My mom always has a stack of books beside her bed. Shirley, my foster mom, was big on the classics.

I read *Wuthering Heights*, *Sense and Sensibility*, and *Gulliver's Travels* from her collection. She even had the original sets of *Nancy Drew* and *The Hardy Boys*.

I remember the day I came across the book *Charlie and the Chocolate Factory* at the school library. A few pages in, I was hooked. That book spoke to me. I identified with Charlie. I checked it out repeatedly because It helped me believe life could be magical. I knew my future would be fantastic if I did the right things.

I fell in love with *The Secret Garden*, *A Wrinkle in Time*, and *Are You There God? It's Me, Margaret*. I never paid attention to what was age-appropriate. I didn't feel like I had a typical childhood. So why should labels matter?

I read voraciously. At one point, someone gave my mom a set of encyclopedias. I decided to read them all. I got up to the letter I when they disappeared. My mom said she donated them, but I felt she sold the set because she needed money.

While visiting my mom, I saw her sticking books on the top shelf in her bedroom. When I got the chance, I climbed up and pulled out the hidden books. The two could not have been more different.

One was a romance by Rosemary Rogers that sent me on a decades-long romance novel spree. That book helped me understand passion and sex. I read what seemed like a million romance novels after that experience.

The other book was Vincent Bugliosi's *Helter Skelter*. Yep, I read that far too young. However, I had already seen so much in life that it didn't upset me, as it helped me understand cults and Charles Manson.

That book also sent me on a decades-long spree with true crime.

I have since read thousands of books. I went through most genres. My favorite thriller writers were Dan Brown, Lee Child, Harlan Coben, Michael Connelly, and Patricia Cornwell.

I had grown up tough and read and wrote enough at work. I didn't need any more reality to creep into my days.

# Chapter 48

## AGE 12, MOM'S

The woods next to our apartment were a great escape. I loved to go there when it was raining. I would swim in the creek and swing from the vines. Climbing trees was a favorite pastime.

That was how I taught myself to do a backflip. I hung upside down and swayed until I got the right speed and flipped backward off the branch.

When it was warm out, I would take my shampoo and wash my hair in the creek. I would give myself facials and mud baths. I may have been a tom-boy, but I always liked spa treatments. I enjoy dipping my whole body in slippery mud.

## SHAMAN ISIS

Once, some girls in my apartment complex went to the woods so I could show them how to spa nature's way. We were having a ball when it started to rain.

We realized that a hill nearby made for a great slide. So we got starker and gave ourselves mud baths, hurling down the slippery slope. It was the most fun I ever had with a group of girls.

When we were good and covered in sludge, we dove into the creek and rinsed off. I remember washing my hair in the rain. It took forever to get the mud out, but it was terrific.

I felt so alive and carefree. I realized that one of the reasons I adventured was to experience the emotions I held when adults were around.

Sometimes, I would collect mud and rainwater and give myself spa treatments in the bathroom. My family thought this was weird. I didn't care.

My two sisters were forever telling me how strange I was. I liked to make up words and phrases. In the early 80s, I nicknamed the TV the boob tube. They were always finding an excuse to show cleavage. I never really understood why men had such a thing for boobs.

I nicknamed the popular hairstyle of the time flybacks. I once watched Jose Eber on TV explaining how he cut Farrah Fawcett's hair. I figured I was decent at spa treatments, so I should be able to copy his technique.

I found scissors in the kitchen and repeated what he did in our bathroom. I remember dropping chunks of hair in the trash, thinking it might upset my mom; I flushed it instead. I will never know why I thought she wouldn't notice what I did.

My mom's face when she saw my hair was worth every minute. First, she asked who cut my hair. She said it was hard to believe when I told her I did. So, I took her to the bathroom and showed her the strands still stuck in the trash.

She didn't even get upset. She seemed impressed. She had me show her how I did it so she could use the same technique to cut my sister's hair.

# Chapter 49

## AGE 12, MOM'S

Animals are something else I love. I would communicate with them like Mister Ed, the talking horse. I realized that animals weren't that different from people. You could usually figure out their thoughts if you paid attention to their energy.

The first dog I was ever around was Hoppy. He was Shirley and Jimmy's dog. Hoppy was a little black and white Lhasa Apso. You could barely see his eyes. I loved Hoppy.

People didn't treat their pets like children in those days. So, when Shirley and Jimmy adopted their first baby, Hoppy disappeared. I thought that was sad.

They had tried to have children for years. She had one false pregnancy and miscarriage after another. That is how I learned that getting attached to an outcome could eat people alive. Shirley was obsessed with getting pregnant. She finally stopped radiating pain when they heard their first baby was ready for adoption from Saint Peter's.

I came home to my Mom's from school one day to find the door window shattered. I thought someone had broken into the apartment. So, of course, I went inside to check it out.

I grabbed a knife from the kitchen drawer and walked around each room. When I got to our bedroom, I noticed a strange energy. I heard funny sounds.

When I got on my knees and moved the bedspread, I found a cat with a full assortment of kittens. The new mom had broken in to give birth. Wow, God had delivered my dream of having a cat right in the bedroom. A gift just for me; I was very excited.

I cuddled those kittens like they were mine. My mom was shocked when she found out. A few days later, she packed the kittens into a box and loaded us into the car. I knew she was crying but didn't want us to see.

She had already warned us that we could not keep the kittens. She could barely feed us. I had hoped that it would work out, but it didn't.

She drove around to the most luxurious subdivision. I remember quietly crying in the back. She took the box holding the mother and kittens and stuck it in front of the big gates. When she returned to the car, she said she had made it impossible for them not to be adopted by a wealthy family.

When we got home, I saw the kitten poster on our bedroom door and started crying again. My heart hurt. I had to make it stop. It was too much.

I was crying for more than just the kittens. I desperately wanted someone to tell me I would have pets and a real home one day.

After that, I taught myself not to feel anything when I saw the poster. That took several days. I would walk up to it and stare until I stopped crying. I stared at it until my heart stopped hurting. Pretty soon, I could stare at it and feel nothing. I was proud of myself.

Not long after, a puppy showed up on our doorstep. I hesitated even to name it. My mom was exhausted from work and didn't have the energy to deal with our new dog.

My sisters named her Elvira. I wouldn't say I liked the name, but the dog was cute. My mom felt bad that her recent promotion kept her away most of the time. She didn't have it in her to take Elvira away. One small puppy was easier to manage than a slew of cats.

Elvira was a bit wild. She would run out the door every time it opened. We had a neighbor who was giving Mom heartburn. I thought of her as the angry fat lady. She complained to us every chance she got about the dog. She would wake my mom just to bitch about the dog running out of the apartment.

She was looking for reasons to get angry. I was starting to get worried about how upset she was getting. It had nothing to do with her! Honestly, I am not sure she would have bothered if my mom had no male admirers.

Mom was very concerned the lady would complain to the office. We were living there against the terms of the lease. She was very stressed that the manager would find out there were three children in our apartment. The lease only allowed two children. I don't think she realized how this affected my sisters. My older sister Deanna was so worried she never left the house. I did not have the same problem.

One day, I was swimming at the pool. I heard the kids yelling my name. When I looked up, I saw the angry neighbor lady standing by the fence with a strange look. My heart sank before she spoke; I knew evil had come to visit our family.

She asked me to come with her because there had been an accident. She said she was so sorry, but it wasn't her fault. I knew she was lying. She could barely keep the maniacal grin from her face. She smelled of triumph. It was making my skin crawl.

I asked her what happened, and she claimed that Elvira had escaped the apartment again and ran in front of her car.

I followed her with increasing dread. She could have knocked on our door, but instead, she came to the pool for me. She wanted me to be the one she told. She tried to hurt me because I was defiant in the face of her complaints. She hated that I would defend our dog.

As we approached her car, I took in the scene. It didn't make any sense. I intuitively knew the accident was fake. The car and dog positions were all wrong.

She told me she would take care of our dog. I said, "No, thank you, I will deal with Elvira." When I went to look her over, I immediately saw a small round hole in her little head. The body had no other scratches or blood. She was lying near the car, dead.

That bitch had shot our dog right in the head. I went rigid with shock and anger. I began shaking from the adrenaline racing through my body. I wanted to beat her to death. I was so upset I made myself sit still. I was staring at the bullet hole and counting to myself.

When I turned around, I told her I knew she was lying. I yelled that I could see Elvira had been shot in the head. She looked shocked. She moved to cover her car window. I ran over to see a gun in the front seat.

I put Elvira in a cardboard box and took her home for burial. Soon after, the lady moved out.

I knew my anger wasn't healthy. It was making my heart hurt. So, I had a long talk with my spirit guides about how to deal with my emotions. My guides made up of my angels, ancestors, and my higher self, helped me understand that anger is how our neighbor became so unhappy.

I finally went to the woods to cry and scream the hatred from my body. I shrieked into the forest until I became hoarse.

The trees comforted me with their ancient energy.

# Chapter 50

## AGE 32, NYC

In 2001, I started my first agency. The NYC economy was struggling, but an acquaintance called and asked if I was interested in doing PR for a luxury eyewear line.

The collection was an over-the-top crystal line produced by a highly respected optical company. So, I said yes.

That is how I started my first business, which I named Vision PR. People assumed it was because of my history in eyewear. It was a secret nod to my intuition.

First, I landed the crystal eyewear account. My team secured them some great press and events. I will be honest; I was impressed with the Imitation of Christ fashion shows we did with PR genius Mandie Erickson. We sponsored several of the shows with Showroom 7 in the early years.

My favorite Imitation of Christ event, with elfin designer Tara Subcoff, occurred at my go-to LA hotel, The Avalon. There were synchronized swimmers right in the middle of the show, which was fantastic.

The client was thrilled at the celebrity turnout. I remember a young Scarlett Johanson. Her hair was cut in a wild mullet. She could have cared less about the paparazzi. I loved that about her. Owen Wilson, Angelica Houston, and Reese Witherspoon also attended. The show made the cover of *People*.

Our work with that first client and a reference from my fashion fairy godmother, Fern Mallis, landed my agency, Silhouette Optical, as a client. They were the parent company and a massive international brand that sponsored fashion week.

They were also the official eyewear provider for the astronauts. The fact that I got to work with people in NASA's space program was a grand slam.

I greatly respect Silhouette, a historical Austrian brand; they invented titanium rimless eyewear frames that revolutionized the optical industry.

My agency now manages the New York Fashion Week sponsorship. That grew to include LA and Miami Fashion Week. We have been doing events worldwide and working with top designers, major award shows, and many celebrities.

We would invite the most influential people in the media and the arts each season to the Silhouette booth in the Bryant Park Tents. My team fit them for the newest collection.

This approach gave Silhouette an even more loyal following. Thousands of global media visited our booth. Our VIP space is a must-visit for the top media, designers, artists, and industry power players.

I used this unprecedented access to implement the first influencer marketing campaigns. In the first few years, we spent much time explaining my concept for influencer marketing. Some thought social media was a trend, and others loved being a billboard in exchange for hot sunglasses.

My fashion fairy godmother, Fern Mallis, founded New York Fashion Week. Now, I get to work with her frequently. She would take me along to events outside the official Bryant Park Tents. Everyone knew who she was. I adored the fact that it never went to her head. She is kind to everyone.

Fashion Week sponsors held tickets to all the shows. That meant seeing my favorite tent designers every season, like Oscar de la Renta, Carolina Herrera, and Zac Posen.

My right arm was a dear friend named Georgio. We worked together at Nadine Johnson and Associates. We had a wonderful time working on Silhouette. She helped me launch the influencer marketing industry.

I was as happy as I had ever been, respected and busy. Although I liked to let my hair down with a few cocktails, I was pretty healthy during these years.

The sponsorships allowed me to indulge in my artistic side. The booth theme and design were always a lot of work. I loved it!

I liked to hide messages in the art. It was my way of flipping my foster parents the bird for withholding my art scholarship. I found out right in the middle of high school graduation. I was surprised to discover I had received two scholarships, one for acting and one for art when the awards were announced during the ceremony.

# Chapter 59

## AGE 36, NYC

It seemed ironic that I would grow up to work with people at NASA. I was a massive fan of space.

Not only was I born the year we landed on the moon, but I was named after Artemis. Cynthia is an epithet of the Greek moon goddess.

My mom said she chose it because she believed I was made of stardust. It turns out she was right; we all are.

I have always believed that humanity's future lies in the cosmos.

Silhouette had a massive celebration for its 40th anniversary. We started working on the event months in advance. It had a generous budget and the full support of the founders.

Guests entered a dramatic, long hallway lined with models in historical clothing and Silhouette eyewear dating back to 1964. I booked a trapeze act to perform over the bar during cocktail hour. Guests then entered the stunning ballroom for the main event.

The decor was one aspect I worked tirelessly creating. I chose a two-story backdrop of black velvet covered in glittering stars. I had the production company make a wall of screens for the stage that split in the middle to allow speakers a grand entrance. We even worked on a space-inspired video to celebrate the anniversary.

The Johnson Space Center sent an astronaut and their chief optometrist to speak at the event. Guests were delighted.

We even had a futuristic virtual reality experience that thrilled the guests. I had a model on a big screen speaking in real-time. Guests thought it was magical. She was in another room wearing an earwig, very Jetson's.

I brought Getty Images to set up a portrait studio in the middle of the ballroom. They took fun photos of the guests wearing historical eyewear from the archives we had on display. We will mail the images as gifts after the event, long before photo booths were popular at events. The photos turned out fantastic.

A book commemorating the anniversary was produced and shared at the event. We showcased it alongside Silhouette magazines from previous decades. I was delighted to see the book included many photos of celebrities my team had placed in Silhouette. This event was one of my all-time favorites.

A few months later, I worked with a female astronaut for Fashion Week's only space-related press conference. I had a ball producing that event.

Astronaut Marsha Ivins was incredible. She handled the event, media, and photographers with ease.

My team collaborated with Pamella Roland on their show again. Models strutted the runway in Silhouette's newest collection. Marsha and I sat in the front row wearing Pamela's stunning dresses. That night, Fern, Marsha, and I hung out on the founders' absurdly beautiful yacht. It was like a dream day.

I remember three things about spending time with the space-trotting icon; she brought me a disk of images taken by the Hubble telescope. I had never seen such beautiful photos. I promised not to share the disk with anyone.

For months, I took the disk out to marvel at space. I even used one as a personal screen saver. Years later, several of those images became famous for just that use.

Secondly, we went to dinner with two men one night, and they repeatedly interrupted us even though we were discussing exciting topics. I was incredulous.

These two men were sitting with the most exciting woman and didn't show the appropriate respect. At one point, one of the men said something dumb, and she slayed him in the most sophisticated way. I was taking notes. We bonded over misogyny.

Lastly, a few weeks after the press conference, Marsha sent me a lovely signed photo of her in space. Her long, curly hair was floating all around her, magnificent.

I was 36 and having a grand time.

# Chapter 52

## AGE 8, THE ORPHANAGE

Sister Anne Elizabeth and I walked through the gardens. Moments like these are a highlight of living at Saint Peter's. She had the most beautiful energy. She glowed like a gold pillar candle.

We talked about life, adults, and religion. She never forced her beliefs on me. She encouraged me to think for myself. She never took opinions personally, something I noticed about many adults.

She was one of the few people who embraced my bluntness. I learned to mask at a young age. My tendency to speak the truth was not welcome. Shirley hated how comfortable I was with adults. I got along well with some and made others uncomfortable.

I would study people to understand what behaviors were appropriate. I would then try on the behavior and add what worked to my closet of characters. I was learning to be a chameleon.

One day, after one of our walks, I snuck out of Saint Peter's, and a young girl followed me. When I realized she was there, I was resigned to having a buddy for the excursion. I did lecture her about the dangers of running around Memphis.

At one point, I noticed a van. They were rare. I had become wary of vehicles because of the number of times I had almost been kidnapped. I was keenly aware that my adventuring was putting me in harm's way.

Before I knew what was happening, that van pulled up next to us, and the door flew open. The men had the scariest looks on their faces. They reeked of booze and bad intentions.

One of them grabbed both of us. I saw restraints, guns, and ropes on the floor. I completely lost it. My temper was something I was not proud of, but at this moment, I allowed myself to become a terror. I was not about to be responsible for someone else getting hurt.

My flailing legs and fists took him by surprise. I dragged the other girl out with me. She was crying. I picked her up and ran back to Saint Peter's.

## SHAMAN ISIS

She was confused about what happened, so I explained that they had mistaken us for kids they knew. How else to distract her from the truth?

That cooled my desire to go adventuring for a while. I was sick of people trying to kidnap me or drag me into a car.

I was glad I knew wonderful boys and foster fathers; otherwise, I might have become a man-hater.

## Chapter 53

### AGE 13, MOM'S

My mother worked nights at a tobacco company. She must have been well-liked because she was constantly given gifts from men and women she managed.

I resented the company for moving her to the night shift. She had three daughters at home. Was that the best they could do with one of their favorite employees? She trained most of the men that she worked under. They were strange times for intelligent women.

My mom wasn't flashy. She had hidden depths. Her family did terrible things to her growing up. So, my mom didn't trust anyone. Once I found out what her mother and stepfather did, I couldn't bring myself to bother with them. Some people don't deserve your time.

Although beautiful in an unconventional way, my mom never saw herself as beautiful. She had striking blue eyes and gorgeous legs. She also had hidden talents.

She could draw what she saw and create complicated three-dimensional art on paper or with an etch-a-sketch. I have never seen anything as mind-blowing as what she drew with two tiny wheels. These were talents she hid from everyone.

I remember when I was young, she had hair three and a half feet off her shoulders. Once, when a tobacco chewing machine jammed, her hair got caught, and the machine ripped a massive chunk out. She cut her hair off after that happened.

Another time, her hand was nearly chewed up when she went to unjam that same machine. I helped her change her bandage, and my knees grew weak looking at the stitches. I could feel the trauma rolling off of her from the accident. After that, I practiced guarding myself against others' pain.

She worked in a dangerous part of Memphis. I worried about her driving so late at night.

The news reported that women were being run off the road late at night by a gang of men. The women were beaten, raped, and terrorized.

## MEMORY MANSION

I was not surprised when we found a gun in her glove box.

My sisters and I found the gun while she was in the store. We were shocked and impressed. My older sister said that it must be from our grandfather. He had given Mom something wrapped in cloth that she had hidden. One of the few good deeds I remember him doing.

I was looking at my mom with new eyes.

Not long after we found the gun, I woke up in the middle of the night. I was dreaming that my mom was being attacked. I saw what happened in my visions. I knew when I woke up that it was serious.

When I heard her come in, I went to the living room. She was oblivious to my presence. She was shaking and holding the gun. She was so scared that it was fused to her hand. I could smell that she had fired the gun. I had to pry it out of her grip.

A carload of men ran her off the road on her way home from work. They surrounded her car and screamed awful things through the crack of her window.

They yelled at her to get out. They said they had guns. She opened the glove box in time to point her gun back out of the window crack.

Those men unloaded a bunch of bullets at her car. The site of all those bullet holes in her door told me how many times she had come close to being shot. She emptied her gun back at them.

I remember the kind policeman who came to our apartment. He was afraid to include the gun in his report because she wasn't supposed to have a weapon. He took the gun with him.

After that, men from the plant gave her rides. She was in this state of mind when I "ran away' from home and made the papers in a spectacular car accident.

# Chapter 54

## AGE 38, NYC

My mom asked me to visit her. It was a strange phone call. She knew that I was not particularly eager to come back to Memphis. I remember how tired she sounded.

When I hung up, I told my husband she didn't sound like herself. She seemed strangely exhausted. He didn't care how she sounded. He had never bothered to get to know my mom.

He has tried to criticize her over the years for the decision to put us in care. I shut that bullshit down with one look every time. My stink eye was notorious.

I learned to control my temper because I had seen what I could do. My last fistfight was so violent it made me ill.

Even though I was defending my family, I was appalled at how quickly I could escalate to someone's worst nightmare. Most deeply empathetic people have a ferocious side you do not want to unleash.

My partner's mother was a lovely woman who spoiled him to compensate for how verbally abusive his father could be. He was the only boy in his immediate family. So, the rest of the family could be very indulgent.

He spent years love-bombing me. So, when he asked me to marry him, I assumed marriage would include the thoughtful things he did over the years.

I had given up on the idea of romantic love. I didn't realize I was sapiosexual until years later. The only super-intelligent men I met were in relationships. What can I say? I was thirty and trying to be practical when I decided to get married.

I remember dinner with my boss, Jamie, before the wedding. I told him that I was worried because our conversations were not stimulating. I was concerned that we didn't have enough in common. I was not listening to my intuition or my spirit guides. I had let my ego take over my life.

Jamie reminded me that my fiance was intelligent, tall, handsome, and fit. He modeled for GNC and had a solid family and career. He did have a lot of positive attributes. So what if he wasn't into books, art, or architecture?

My new husband didn't even make it to the honeymoon before he let his dark side show. I regretted the marriage immediately. It was too late. I was not about to get divorced again. If I handled him correctly, he would grow—famous last words.

Everyone thought I had won the lottery, the local Ken and Barbie. Little did they know how toxic the relationship would become. The longer we were together, the more horrendous we behaved. When it got bad, I escaped to the bathroom. As the years passed, my escapist behavior worsened.

My mother has been dealing with health issues for years. She had diabetes and celiac. I wish I had been more understanding of how she felt. Later, I realized that her unhealed trauma was one of the main things that made her sick.

I was in my office at Escada when I got the call. It was a nurse from a Memphis hospital. She informed me that my mom was dying, and I needed to come home immediately.

Mom told me once that she was afraid to marry again while she still had daughters at home. I understood that she feared what some men could hide about themselves. That is why she chose to remain single for years.

So, I was very disappointed when she finally married a loser who used her terribly. Returning to Memphis was scary enough; I found every excuse not to visit once he joined the picture.

Now, I am speechless. I could not believe what I was hearing. I knew mom was sick, and my younger sister was concerned. She has been struggling for years.

I did not expect her to pass away in my late 30s. I cried the whole way back to Memphis. I felt terrible for the people on the plane. I was so worried that she would die before I got to see and touch her again.

When we got to the hospital, I ran to her room. I was shocked when I saw her. She was severely bloated and very pale. She said, "Cindy, is that you?" I said it was. She said, "Good, I waited for you. I love you, honey." Those were the last words my mother spoke.

My older sister Deanna rolled her eyes and huffed out of the hospital room. I could tell she was high on crack. She had been a crack addict and prostitute for years.

I was deeply ashamed of her lifestyle. The crack had turned Deanna into a shell of the sister I knew. I always thought her choices were partly to blame for my mother's health issues.

Mom tried everything to help Deanna. We dragged her out of more than one crack den over the years.

## MEMORY MANSION

I was devastated when the intensive care nurse told me my mother should not be dying at such a young age. She added that she would have survived septicemia if given proper antibiotics in time.

My mom had tried to get help, but her complex history made hospital doctors tell her to see her doctor. By the time she did see him, it was too late.

That still happens to women all the time. They seek healthcare for specific symptoms only to be dismissed. I stopped going to the doctor for years due to having my health concerns dismissed.

I asked the nurse how much time Mom had left. Even though I already knew it wasn't very long. She said it could be hours.

My husband wanted to leave the hospital and wait in a hotel room for "the call." I could not believe he demanded that I leave the hospital, knowing my mother could die any minute. I said I would get my carry-on from the car. I was going to sleep at the hospital.

We argued in the parking lot. It got nasty. He was acting like this was all an inconvenience. I had already concluded that we were not going to last much longer. Now, I knew it was going to end badly.

While we were arguing, I heard my younger sister yelling at me. She was saying that Mom only had a few minutes.

So, instead of being by her side in her remaining time, I was arguing in the parking lot. I was disgusted. Selfishness didn't even begin to cover what I thought of his behavior.

I ran inside and got to her bed just in time to feel her spirit leave her body. I was incandescent and devastated.

I felt like a horrible daughter for not visiting her.

This experience began a dark chapter in my life; I was about to lose control of everything.

A part of me was glad she was not alive to see the mess I would make of my life.

# Chapter 55

## AGE 17, COLLIERVILLE

High School was a ball. MTV dominated the trends. The music was incredible. My home life may have been weird, but school was excellent. I was introverted but friendly with everyone.

People used to say I got on with the jocks, freaks, heads, and popular kids. That made me proud. I tried hard not to judge anyone. I knew what that was like.

I played volleyball, was on the yearbook staff, and enjoyed going to classes for a change. I even got involved in theater. I remember being in *Up The Down Staircase*. My audition was fun. That is when I realized that years of masking made me good at improving. I took people by surprise.

The art classes were great. I learned to draw, paint, sculpt, and make ceramics. My teacher gave me a bulletin board to display my artwork. The local paper took a photograph of me standing before my work. I was very proud to have turned my life around. I still gave speeches to kids about making the right choices.

I was close with several teens from my church. We spent a lot of time together. Some of the best memories I have are of going to camp with all the kids. Shirley was there, of course.

I wanted to tell my friends what was happening at home but was afraid of what would happen to me. I was tough but scared. I never understood how it all pieced together. I was followed by people who were organized and prepared. I had also been threatened, taunted, and almost kidnapped many times.

People had noticed how "overprotective" my foster father was. He threatened several boys over the years. Someone once said, "Are they saving you for some powerful man? Haha". My mom and I wondered if they were part of a cult.

Jimmy threw one boy against the dining room wall to warn him about ever touching me. He gripped one of my best friends and squeezed him painfully for talking to me during church service. He grabbed another friend by his shirt and scared him pasty. Several times, he lost control of his temper in front of others.

A few people had noted that he acted like a jealous boyfriend. They laughed it off, but I wasn't laughing. I found his behavior disturbing enough without people knowing the truth. He had been watching me through peepholes and spies for years. I could feel his stare. I went to great trouble to get dressed without being observed.

Occasionally, strange men would come to the house to look at me. It always creeped me out. I got furious about it once and lost control of my mouth. My foster parents often made me wear baggy clothes. Shirley bought size twelve for me even though I was thin.

One day, Jimmy gave me an outfit to try on. I was surprised because it was a cute sleeveless top and short shorts.

That is when Jimmy called me outside to meet someone. He would claim it was someone from work. He then called to the bottom of the driveway.

They were watching me too closely. A man in a suit was sitting in the back of a long car. Jimmy and another man were standing by the front of the vehicle. He asked me to take a turn. I got irritated and asked what the show was about.

Jimmy turned red and told me to be polite to the guests. They were looking at me like merchandise. It creeped me

SHAMAN ISIS

out. I abruptly turned and went back inside. I could feel eyes on my body the entire way.

The outfit disappeared after that.

# Chapter 56

## AGE 16, COLLIERVILLE

Kroger was the biggest grocery store in town. I got a job there for extra money. Of course, Jimmy liked to show up unannounced to check on me.

I had a great time working at the store. It gave me a way to meet lots of different people. I liked to people-watch.

I could be goofy at work. We would pull stunts on each other, such as asking for a price check on tampons through the intercom.

One day, when I went to clock in, there was a note stuck to my time card. It was from one of the assistant managers. He invited me to go bowling with some of the staff. I tucked the note in my bag and forgot about it.

A few days later, one of the women on staff hurled a register tray at me. Change flew everywhere. She had tears in her eyes. I was stunned. What did I do to upset her? Well, I was about to find out.

I was called on the inner store phone. It was the assistant manager. He wanted to know what had happened to cause a detective to approach him on the street. He was warned about the danger of hitting on underage girls. The detective knew many details about his personal life.

The assistant manager was freaked out. He was amidst a bad breakup and didn't need the drama. He begged me not to tell anyone about the phone call. He just wanted me to know how serious the situation was. His girlfriend was upset because they threatened his livelihood: his girlfriend, the woman who had thrown a metal tray at me.

I knew what had happened. I got my purse out and looked for the note from my time card. It was gone.

I confronted Jimmy when I got home. He enjoyed bragging about the detective who looked into my assistant manager at work. He also rattled off the details of my movements since I brought the note home. I didn't understand how he could have caused all these problems so quickly.

He did not have the means to have a police detective or any detective on the payroll.

It was these moments that scared me the most. I didn't always know when I was being followed.

## Chapter 57

## AGE 36, NYC

*WWD*, a fashion trade magazine, had a position listed with a brand I wanted to work with. They were looking for someone who could build a celebrity following.

I knew I would regret closing Vision PR. However, I saw my future, and dressing celebrities for awards shows was part of my journey.

Escada is a famed German fashion house that I remember dressing Kim Basinger for her LA Confidential Oscar. I knew other fashion houses would take issue with my lack of a degree and thought this fashion house might accept my unique experience instead of a degree. They did.

In 2005, I took on my most significant challenge with a brand close to home. They needed someone who could reinvent and reignite the brand, not only in the US but around the world.

I was breathless after reading the role's description. Since working with Fern at Robert Marc, I have wanted to prove myself at a fashion house. Putting a dated brand back on the map was a challenge I dreamed of taking on. I was not surprised when they responded to my resume. I have manifested the opportunity.

I knew I had the necessary product when I saw their gowns and accessories. Add to that my experience and street smarts, and I knew I could pull it off.

Escada had not dressed anyone of note in years, and I knew I could make them hot again.

A few days before I officially started, I got the princess treatment. One of the advantages of being the mouthpiece for an expensive fashion house is the clothing allowance. My position required me to wear the brand to all press interviews, meetings, and events. So, before starting my new role, I was sent to the flagship store on 5th Avenue for a shopping spree. I smiled when I saw Robert Marc around the corner.

I have to be honest; walking into a luxury store with an endless budget is something every woman should get to experience. The enormous boutique was the jewel of their American stores and had the best stylists.

They greeted me like the star I would be in the company. It was a magical experience trying on exquisite suits, cocktail dresses, and ball gowns. I had good taste and made the most of the opportunity. I selected a beautiful new wardrobe and added shoes and handbags to the pile.

A tailor was fetched to fit all my new clothing. Hours later, I left the store with dozens of enormous shopping bags. I wouldn't say I liked shopping, but that made me feel like Cinderella on her way to the ball.

It was time to get down to business.

It was more challenging than I expected, and not for business reasons. There was a lot of gossip and backstabbing. I was treated horribly by several of the other executives, no matter what magic I worked. I was used to this in the luxury world, especially in NYC.

No matter how big the ROI. No matter the celebrity's fame, I was not "good enough" for that job or title. They had the biggest problem with my brown hair and olive skin, which surprised me the most.

It was so bad that I had to turn the team over in the first few months. Simply because they didn't believe I, nor the brand, had what it took. Worse, in my eyes, they didn't think it was possible. An insecure executive had poisoned the pool. These were not people who understood the force of personality.

One of my assistants said straight to my face, 'You should be blonde and from a society family.' Wow, in 2005?! None of them lasted long in the face of my defiance.

I could handle them not believing in me; I enjoyed proving people wrong. What they said about the brand opened the door to changing the entire team. So, I did.

If you do not believe something is possible, do everyone and yourself a favor and leave. You are poisoning your brand or company. If you can say that you do not believe better is possible at any job, you are bad for business and the team's mental health.

"What are you?" was a frequent question growing up. I've heard that my whole life. It is how people who want to know your heritage find out what they can. Not everyone does it for that reason. These folks had an unhealthy fascination with my race. A legacy I didn't know.

While my husband was beloved for his connections and accomplishments (his degree and Franklin Lakes-based family), my family and history had to be a mystery.

I didn't want anyone to learn about my life because they would use it against me. I could not tell my partner the truth because he didn't understand that personal information was ammunition in business. So, I stuck with my plan.

I decided that all events for the brand and stores would support a charity, museum, or humanitarian organization. My new, hand-selected team and I created over one hundred annual local and experiential events to support the community and drive awareness. We were breaking new ground in authenticity and brand activism.

We did everything from intimate client dinners to national charity events. I replaced the seasonal fashion show with a fundraiser for Saint Jude Children's Research Hospital, a nod to my hometown.

I also continued to leverage my position to encourage sustainability and reusability. One of my most successful opportunities came when I got Katherine Heigl into a stunning vintage gown at the Emmy Awards.

I knew the nude and silver sequin dress I brought back on my lap from Germany would tip Katherine into style-darling while highlighting reusability.

The smoldering look was celebrated across entertainment TV and made the covers of *People*, *US*, and *USA Today*. She was named the best-dressed woman that evening. The keywords for her dress were the 2nd most searched the following day on Google. My CEO and the German founder were thrilled.

We did it. My team created the most successful program in the company's history. The results were so powerful that they influenced the brand's global success. I received two promotions over the coming months.

## Chapter 58

## AGE 38, NYC

After my mother passed away, I returned to work. I wasn't given much choice. My boss, the CEO, called me during her funeral to find out when I was coming back. Oh, that isn't why he claimed to be calling. However, that was the reason he called. Why else, ask?

I also suddenly had the desire to become a mother. By all means, let's make life more complicated.

I realize how ridiculous it sounds, but I was in my late thirties and thought my marriage would become more civil if we had a child. It would allow me to exit the relationship with less drama. Yes, not one of my wiser moments.

I waited until I was five months pregnant to say anything to my boss. Not sure who I thought I was fooling. He had a note in his hand that said "I'm pregnant" on it. The message was ready to be turned over when I fessed up. He was not happy about my pregnancy but hid it well.

Women were not treated well when they chose to have children in corporate America. So, I timed it with excellent results.

Our results were always staggering. We topped ourselves every time. I was exhausting myself to get bigger and better results.

I commuted four hours a day and worked at least fourteen. I was proud to sleep with my phone in my hand. Seriously, how deluded.

My husband was neither supportive nor understanding about anything but the money I brought home. His social life, friends, and my income were always priorities. My mental, physical, and emotional health didn't seem to register. I should have forced them to be a priority.

He had a driving need to use every hour of the day. I felt terrible for being the breadwinner. So, I let myself be pressured into going out when I was on the verge of collapse. He knew I was exhausted and didn't care. I no longer felt safe in the relationship.

Anyway, I had more giant sharks to deal with. The iconic fashion house founder was being pushed out of the picture. He was a big supporter.

I could foresee that they would push the designer out in favor of some young idiot they could control. Worse, a new man had started working for the main office in Germany. He didn't like me, but he couldn't argue with my results. My intuition was telling me that he was a big problem. When I was promoted twice in one year, he showed me how much trouble he would become.

He tried telling me what celebrities I should work with. He had nothing nice to say about my work. Even though he used photos of every superstar, I dressed in his results presentation to resounding applause.

He asked me several times about my background and heritage. His lips permanently curled during these conversations. I wanted to slap his blond-haired, blue-eyed face.

Occasionally, he would make digs about thinking a blond-haired heiress should have filled my role. An affliction of the mind I already dealt with in America.

Then he pressured me only to put our gowns on white women with blond hair. He knew the programs I built in America were causing a brand revitalization worldwide. He thought he could improve it by limiting the women to one race.

It was always on my tongue to point out how racist that sounded from a German executive. He was an insufferable snob with dated ideas. I stood firm in my beliefs.

He began to pressure me in an abusive manner. My American boss was such an ass-kisser that he did nothing to stop what was happening. He was too busy entertaining his mistress, who was promoted for sleeping with him.

A few months after the pressure started, I flew to Germany for a meeting. We are going over strategy and the red-carpet gown collection.

During one sit-down, my nemesis showed photos of Indian beaders rushing to make new awards show gowns. I remember being sick over how emaciated the beaders were.

He asked me to show the photos to the fashion media to promote the awards show design process. I was shocked. These people were starving.

I asked if we were paying them properly to rush the gowns. No one answered, so I kept asking until I made everyone sufficiently uncomfortable. I may not love confrontation, but I have never had trouble picking up the bat for other people.

We should have paid them what the gowns were worth to our customers. I thought this was sick behavior. The class system celebrated, yuck.

My enemy took grave exception to me embarrassing the men by asking those questions. The silence at that moment made me realize I had crossed an invisible line.

He took me to his office and said some of the awful things I had ever heard one human being say to another at work. He was furious with me and took issue with my disgusting childhood and "mixed-race" background.

My family didn't know what we were, and I had never had the nerve to ask my mother if my father was mixed-race. Growing up, I heard many rumors about his heritage. It was clear she didn't know. So, why bring up something she could not answer?

My nemesis was angry at how unsuitable I was for my job. He turned red, and spit flew from his lips as he said he would ruin my career if I didn't do what he demanded.

From then on, he told me I had better dress only white women with blonde hair. I remember throwing out some famous names; no one was good enough.

I couldn't do what he demanded. It was racist and ignorant.

I remember thinking, 'Is he going to say it out loud?'" and he did. He was dead serious about only working with blond-haired white women.

He had never come out and explicitly said not to dress anyone other than white women with blond hair. Now, he was making that known. The only exception was a brunette Academy Award winner or nominee.

He asked me again about my race.

He could not believe someone of my "revolting background" ever got such a high-profile job. I will never know how he discovered my history. He used my shock to his advantage.

I wanted to scream, "High profile job! I made it a high-profile job!" but he couldn't see it.

Anyway, bam, there IT was! One of my greatest fears came true in the most brutal way possible. An industry that I loved and gave my heart and soul to, and I still "wasn't good enough." It was devastating.

The worst part of this experience was that I was visibly pregnant during this insane conversation. This asshole was also fully aware that my mother had recently and unexpectedly died.

He wanted to give me a breakdown. He came close to accomplishing that goal with the help of my shame and fear.

I was far more traumatized than I realized. I had an epic case of imposter syndrome. Not only did I feel like an imposter for running from my past and not using my real name, but I made it where few people believed I could.

My nemesis didn't see that the diversity of the people we were dressing was responsible for blowing the brand up. That was my mistake. See, I learned this the hard way. Elitists are afraid for everyone to have access to better. It threatens the hierarchy from which they derive self-esteem.

I let this racist climb inside my head while he imploded my life. First, he terrorized me while I was trying to have a family. He took my maternity leave away, and he set me up. He wanted me to be weak and voiceless.

I could not believe he had all this personal information about me.

Not long after that, I was at a Metropolitan Museum of Art gala. I was leaving the museum in my glorious lace gown and Harry Winston earrings (on loan) when a taxi bumper caught the back of my dress and ripped it in two. I knew right then what was coming my way, which was terrifying.

Why me? I had never told my husband my real story. For one, I was ashamed. Two, because he loved sharing what he knew with everyone. He has zero filters.

As this horrible businessman was crushing my maternity leave, I knew everything would change.

They forced me to return to work right after having my son. I spent a week in the hospital while my beautiful son was in the NICU. I had negotiated a four-month leave. I was supposed to work from home during that time. They took those months away and forced me to commute four hours daily while newly breastfeeding or not being paid.

They were aware that I was the breadwinner. They used that to steal months of precious memories.

My fellow executives had smelled the way the wind was blowing and ran for cover. Not one person said a word about what they did to me. Not one person responsible for protecting my maternity leave could find a way to speak up.

I sought legal advice. My fancy lawyer told me I had a serious lawsuit that would not pay the bills for years. He was very upset about my case. He had seen this before. I was forced to negotiate an exit deal that allowed them to pretend I was still running the department for a long time.

I would apologize for hating them, but that was my son, mother, career, and life.

# Chapter 59

## AGE 40, NY

My mother's death, crumbling marriage, and imploding career were what finally began to send me off the rails. I had been running for years. First, I ran from Jimmy and Company. Then, I ran from my past. I was about to start running from myself.

I have been dancing close to depression and addiction for years. My identity was my work. I did not know how to function without it. My mother was gone, and my unhealthy marriage tied up all my other relationships. I had no one to talk to who knew the truth or my history. I was incapable of telling anyone about my real past.

Like any toxic relationship, my husband poured on the razzle-dazzle for my friends. I had noticed his need to be friends with my friends but mistook it for caring. He also chased off people who cared for me, especially people who didn't like him. He just wanted to control my life and our narrative. I was too busy with work to care.

I asked for a divorce while pregnant and still living with him. That was a huge mistake. I should have run while he was out of town. I was trying to get away with some of the investments I had made in our marriage, another huge mistake.

I should have known the lengths he would take to ensure he made out like a prince. I never told any of our friends or family what happened, and I never will.

I was trying to deal with everything, but being in negative energy attracts horrible life experiences. It was about to get much worse.

After hanging out with friends one night, I left my son belted and sleeping in his bouncy cradle. The portable bed was his favorite place to sleep. I left the baby monitor by him and went to bed.

I was awoken a little while later by heavily armed police swarming the house. I will be honest. Their behavior terrorized me. I was aware that I had complex PTSD, and this just made it worse.

They were screaming at me like criminals. I watched them from my bedroom doorway as they riffled through my house and shook their heads judgmentally at a tasteful book of nudes on my coffee table. Were they the morality police? I also watched them dig through my trash. I was sure all of it was illegal.

They were acting as though they had come across the scene of something terrible. I came down the stairs and asked what the hell was going on.

Someone had called them anonymously and reported a baby alone in the house. Well, that was impossible. Not only was I there, but the place was elevated two stories off the ground without a line of sight to my son.

When the police arrived at my home, they didn't see the sign beside the doorbell explaining it didn't ring. So, they stormed in like the anonymous call was fact instead of fiction. They finally left.

A few days later, I got a call that I needed to come to the police station. I was going to be arrested for being too far from my son. I was shocked to be told they were calling it child endangerment. WTF, I was 20 feet away and had a baby monitor on.

I suspected my husband or work nemesis had gotten creative. My fancy lawyer told me I had been arrested for one reason: to prevent me from suing the police department for entering my home illegally.

## MEMORY MANSION

My husband was mortified and secretly delighted. Here was all the ammunition he needed to turn into an absolute beast.

This was the incident. The horrific experience that sent me careening over the edge. I had not slept more than one to two hours at a clip for decades. I could not remember the last time I had dreamed.

Now, I began to have night terrors so horrifying that I did not sleep for over a year; the few minutes I did get were with my eyes wide open. I had nightmares so scary that I left all the lights on.

I began to drink heavily. I became incredibly self-destructive. I was imploding and did not know how to stop.

Finally, I got arrested for something I did.

I tried rehab. That would give me a break from my toxic home situation. I didn't understand the lengths he would go to.

I secretly brought two recovery coach couples into my home to watch my relationship. They both explained that my husband's controlling behavior and deeply hidden anger would destroy me and my relationship with my son if I stayed.

I was scared that I would not survive anyway. So, I finally moved out.

SHAMAN ISIS

My ex had the family and job to care for our son's needs.

One thing he did surprise me with was just how good of a father he was. That made finally leaving easier.

I will add that he did eventually change and grow into a good father and husband. I credit that to his wonderful second wife, Lisa. She was a godsend to our small family.

# Chapter 60

## AGE 12, MOM'S

I love music. I have always enjoyed most styles of music. My mom adored '70s bands like the Eagles, Foreigner, and Fleetwood Mac. Shirley loved the classics and Broadway. That exposure gave me diverse tastes in genres.

I learned to play the guitar. I would hang out with friends and play rock music. Several of the kids were in bands that competed in Battle of the Bands. Teens turned backyards into mini-stages for concerts. It was awesome. All my closest guy friends had hair longer than mine.

I practiced guitar in Elvis' backyard, well, close enough. My friend Anne lived in one of the only houses that bordered Graceland. She is a beautiful soul and was a great pianist. We played church music and soft rock hits.

We would venture to her back fence and watch whoever was hanging out in Graceland's backyard.

My constant proximity to Graceland is how I would meet Elvis again. I was out running the streets when I found myself amid a stream of people. The sun was in my eyes. When it cleared, I stood before the "mayor."

Our encounter was extraordinary.

Elvis radiated pain and sadness. I was unsure if he recognized me, but he seemed to feel he knew me. He touched my young head, and a white light filled me. He was communicating through touch and energy.

When Elvis passed soon after, I cried for several days.

In my early teens, I snuck out to concerts with friends. I would roll towels in my bed and sneak out via the roof.

My first concert was STYX, the Mr. Roboto tour. That concert was strange because I went with a friend and his father. The whole time, I was getting heavy feelings from my friend's dad. The speakers and the busy environment made my head spin. We eventually left early.

The father committed suicide a few couple of days later. That is when I understood what I was feeling was his hopelessness. I filed that experience away; I didn't want to be confused over that state in the future. I might be able to give someone hope.

The next concert was life-changing. I went to see KISS. They were in costume and giving rock-god vibes. I appreciated their polished show. They knew how to get an arena in the palm of their hands.

I saw Poison, Ozzy, Motley, and others before I moved to the burbs. After that, I couldn't go to "evil" rock concerts.

I dressed as Nancy Wilson did in the early days of Heart. I loved boots, tight pants, and cool tops. I wore oversized blouses with fat belts and leg warmers. I have always loved makeup and fashion. I don't like to shop, but I like fun clothes.

One benefit of such a weird life is that I got to test-drive most styles.

I went full-on prep when I moved in with my foster parents. I wasn't given much choice, so I made the most of it. Permed hair, bows, and lace collars, ouch.

In college, I became a fan of fashion magazines. I went to three salons before I found someone to cut my long hair off. I wanted Linda Evangelista's short boy cut. I loved her hair and attitude. Strangely enough, my long-term boyfriend hated my short hair, but a new type of guy started looking at me. They were intelligent and independent thinkers.

After college, I slowly shifted to the Southern Gothic style, followed by alternative rock. I have worn it all and had every hair color under the sun.

Right before I ran from Tennessee, I colored my hair light blonde. I didn't want to travel to California looking like "Cindy."

It is strange to see how different clothes, haircuts, and colors affect other people's behavior.

Style certainly alters the way we act. Such as, being dressed nicely makes people more confident.

So, imagine looking like a different person. It certainly helps when you are on the run. It's also a fun way to change up your life experience.

## Chapter 69

### AGE 50, SOUTH FLORIDA

One day, my hair turned white from the stress. For two years, I worked on my sustainable fashion collection named Intention. I was committed to showing the fashion industry that you can make beautiful, investment-quality, eco-clothing in America.

None of the major luxury brands were genuinely committed to the planet. Only Eileen Fisher had some eco-pieces in her collection. However, at the time, even that brand was not sustainable.

I remember discussing sustainability years ago with my good friend, fashion designer Carlton Jones, and his husband, Michou Jones. We were in Jamaica for a fashion event. We were still determining how sustainable fashion would happen, but we knew it was necessary.

My mother had taught me about investment dressing. Before she passed, we discussed the lack of manufacturing in America and how products were produced with planned obsolescence. We came up with the idea of me one day starting a collection and finally sharing my truth. This conversation was before I made a mess of my life.

Years after that conversation and long after my last battle with addiction, I would get to do what we discussed.

After one too many traumas and nearly drinking myself to death, I now live quietly in Florida. I started a new agency with my best friend, Gerard. The agency became successful. Later, we wanted to do something to help further the conversation on sustainability. So, we decided to show the fashion industry that you could make an eco-collection in the US.

Gerard and I have worked with some great luxury brands. Our Miami-area agency, the first brand communications agency in the world, specializes in American brands and products manufactured in the US. Doing a small collection in the States would be easier for me than most people (har har).

Finally, I got the chance to design a fashion collection. I committed to making it sustainable and producing it in

America. It is expected to be one of the first sustainable brands in the country.

I was bloody from the battle to create the line two years in. Few apparel companies knew anything about making sustainable clothing. So, I had to become an expert. Not to mention, there were a lot of sleazy vendors to dig through.

I always know when I am being lied to - it is not fun at work or home. The production company's constant lies were infuriating.

I will be honest. It was one of the most challenging projects I ever took on.

The coronavirus shut the world down as we were finally ready to sew clothing. My custom-made fabric was cut and just sitting in LA. All the work and money invested was "for nothing."

I was getting angry about the whole situation. I couldn't understand how people became cattle overnight. I have always believed, and my intuition agrees, that the coronavirus situation reeked to high heaven. It was a power play and grossly exaggerated.

From the beginning, it was nothing but a financial bonanza for the most influential companies in the world. I was shocked that I could not get anyone to talk rationally about what was happening. It was as if most of us lost the ability to think critically.

People became afraid to speak their minds. That scared me more than anything.

Watching years of work go to waste tipped me into the kind of fury that has to find an outlet. I had been quietly depressed and overweight for ten years. Now, on top of that, I was scared and pissed.

What was happening? Did no one remember thalidomide babies? Why was the media not talking about vaccine history? Why were authorities calling them vaccines when they could not meet the standards?

People were being pitted against each other by the world's most influential people and companies. Watching everyone put through this play for control of humanity was terrifying.

Simultaneously, with the collection's launch and the coronavirus, I committed to being honest about my life experiences. The closure delay was making that commitment increasingly stressful.

I had never told anyone almost anything of my real story. Only my friend and business partner Gerard knew the roughest of details. Now, I was going to share the complete truth. Had I lost my mind?

Then, I was shocked to realize my hair had suddenly turned white. I was so stressed about the collection and

## MEMORY MANSION

talking about my history that my hair turned silver nearly overnight.

My mind, body, and soul were screaming for freedom.

## Chapter 62

## AGE 40, NEW YORK

My sister Deanna and I started speaking again. My battles with addiction and depression had cracked open the door to our relationship. I had one rule: we could not talk if she were high.

She tried very hard to stick to that request.

I was so secretive about my battles that it never occurred to me to get on the phone with anyone. Our calls worked out well most of the time.

Deanna had been a Memphis-area prostitute for years. I was not very sympathetic to her choices. I spent a long time trying to help her, even dragging her out of deadly situations several times. She would go back to using drugs.

I was disgusted after watching her put my mom through hell. Although she was brilliant, I thought of her as weak. I thought of her as someone who just liked to party. That is what GenX was taught to think about addiction.

The truth is that addiction is about unhealed trauma. We have prisons filled with people who have unhealed trauma. How we treat traumatized people makes everything worse for everyone.

Telling traumatized people to "just say no" was devastating to GenX. It laid shame and guilt where it didn't belong. It also implied people were defective for self-medicating their trauma. Trauma that our boomer parents did not want to hear about.

Not to mention that drugs had become easy, cheap, and highly addictive right when mass media began to train us all to live in fear.

During these conversations with Deanna, our past would finally make more sense.

While I had been fortunate enough to escape Jimmy and company unmolested, my sister had not.

He and some other men had destroyed her innocence as a child. While I could hide children from the men entering Saint Peter's, my sister had not been so fortunate. So, it was a ring of men.

It was crushing to hear that while I had been able to help other children, I could not help my sister.

I can remember when Deanna changed. She became hard. Her eyes shimmered with anger.

I stored that moment in memory mansion. It happened before I snuck to see my sister. That time, they took me by the ear to the whipping post. I remember Deanna's eyes took my breath away. It reminded me of the movie *The Body Snatchers*. The young girl I knew was gone. In her place was a bitter stranger.

A few years before my mother died, we talked about Jimmy. He had also hounded my mom for years. He would show up at her work or home and try to hurt her. I knew he was obsessed with the woman in my family. I didn't realize how bad it was until it was too late.

Deanna finally fessed up about getting me sent to juvenile prison at 13. She had been telling lies about me and my antics for months. Oh, I was no angel. I was a bit of a rebel, but I had a good heart.

She also admitted to getting me kicked out of our home, made a ward of the state, and forced me to live with Shirley and Jimmy.

That was hard to hear. My sister knew what he was capable of and still sent me there. She said that she knew I could handle him.

I could not bring myself to tell her how bad it had gotten. Being followed and watched makes you hypervigilant in the extreme. I may have run for years, but that experience paled compared to what she endured.

She had always longed for our father in a way I didn't understand. It created a strange dynamic that men took advantage of.

Warm phone calls were now possible because we were both trying to recover from trauma. We talked about our lives, choices, and family history. We forgave each other and others. We laughed, and we cried.

Months after we reconnected, I got a call I had been expecting for decades. Deanna was found naked in the front yard of a crack house with blood pouring down her legs. I knew right away that she was dying. She was 42.

My intuition had been telling me for months that something was wrong. The edge had left Deanna's voice, and she seemed desperate for a family connection. She even made fun of being so hard on me all those years. She used to joke that she gave me a glamorous life in NYC. In a way, she was right.

For months, I had been having nightmares of her screaming in pain. I did ask if she was sick, and she claimed she was okay.

After we confirmed she was dying, I asked if she knew. She said she had given up trying to get help months beforehand. Everyone thought she just wanted drugs.

Prostitutes and addicts have historically been treated like yesterday's trash, even though I have yet to meet one who was not, first and foremost, a victim.

I went to spend time with her. It was one of the most horrible times of my life. I was back in a town that had a lot of bad memories. On top of that, I was back for a painful reason.

When I first saw Deanna, I was shocked and sick. She was so thin, haunted, and high. During the first few times, I visited her in several crack dens. She was in full escape mode. Which I frankly understood. The things I saw in those homes broke my heart.

The hardest thing was seeing her eyes. Her face was still stunning, but she had gouged the cornea of her right eye, which was milky white with blindness. It took days to look at her without flinching.

After a few weeks, she accepted that she didn't have long. That is when she finally put the pipe down.

To escape, I decided to see what my old high school friends were up to. I was fat, angry, and spoiling for a fight. Part of me wanted Jimmy to find out I was back.

Going on social media to find my old friends is how I found out that people thought I was dead. There were posts about my disappearance and likely death.

It's not every day you read about your demise. I knew people talked about my disappearance but didn't realize some of my closest friends assumed I was dead.

Deanna still had time for cruelty but quickly realized that these would be our last memories.

So, we became like young sisters again. We talked, laughed, cried, colored our hair, got dressed up, and did each other's makeup. She was still a knockout, kidney tubes and all.

The pain she was in was terrible. Her drug tolerance was too high for medication to help. She needed a pain drip, but they refused to provide one for her final months.

The state did everything in its power not to support her when she needed it most. Their treatment of her was one of the hardest things I have ever witnessed.

Her drug tolerance meant she screamed and cried all night. Hearing her was enough to make me lose my mind. I could feel pain, fear, anxiety, and depression rolling off her in huge waves that took my breath away.

Her death tipped me into a prolonged depression. It was just one too many traumas for this old girl to handle. I have not caught a break in years.

SHAMAN ISIS

I was finally in enough pain to begin the long journey to self-love and wellness.

# Chapter 63

## AGE 51, SOUTH FLORIDA

If scars make people tough, I must be one badass bitch. I am covered in them. It took me a long time to realize my external scars have nothing on my internal ones. Those take much more work to heal.

I have crisscross burn marks on one arm from a 70s-era floor heater. As a baby, I was pushed off the top of a slide and bounced chin-first off the concrete. I would go on to bust my chin two more times.

I have fractured my wrists, ankles, feet, fingers, right hip, and two front teeth. Those two teeth came out right after I finally launched the Intention collection! No joke, it took four months to fix because of the coronavirus. Talk about ego-breaking!

I've had hundreds of stitches over the years and have had two permanent indentations on both sides of my pelvis from hitting the handlebars in one of my motorcycle accidents.

Right after getting separated, I shattered my leg doing axles on my rollerblades. It would take nearly seven years to stop limping. I have lost count of how many car accidents I have been in.

Years after being forced to return to work right after a complicated labor, I had to have a dozen hernias repaired. I nearly destroyed my stomach trying to meet the demand to get super fit and thin quickly. I walked around with all those holes in my abdominal wall for years because many doctors don't listen to women. The list goes on and on.

All that pales compared to the healing I would do to recover from a lifetime of trauma and running. First, I ran from Jimmy and his sick group of men. I ran from my childhood by masking my way into a career no undiagnosed autistic woman would find ideal. In recent years, I have been running from myself and my mistakes.

Who was I? I had never even used my real name. More importantly, who was I without my glam career? My career was my identity.

How was I going to begin to unpack everything that I had never talked about?

I was scared to open up. There were so few people left. I had almost no family or friends. It felt like getting naked in front of everyone.

Why did what others think of me even matter? What would happen if I shined a light on my closet full of characters? Would people think I was fake for not being able to be myself? Would they like the real me? Would I?

How in God's name was I even going to get started? It felt like I was at the bottom of a mile-long well without a rope or ladder. I was afraid to begin climbing. It was a long way up, but I could see the sun shining at the top. It was telling me to be brave.

I stood before the mirror and looked at myself for a long time. I had not looked deeply in a mirror for over ten years. I had some tough conversations that day.

Finally, I decided to change everything about myself and my lifestyle one step at a time. I had to learn to love myself and my past.

I had to heal. I had to step out from behind the shame that had kept me quiet for so long. It has been over 40 years since I started keeping secrets.

It was time to open memory mansion. Your secrets keep you sick, after all.

First, I would sleep for the first time in many years.

# Chapter 64

## AGE 51, SOUTH FLORIDA

When I woke up the next day, I was a teenager again. It is hard to describe the powerful change that overcame me. I felt alive like I did when I ran rooftops.

I was no longer hungry. My body was screaming for water and a break from food. I began a long fast that required no discipline. Where was that skill my whole life?

I wanted to go for a walk in the sunshine. It felt glorious. I could not remember the last time I tried to be outside. I needed the sun. It had always been so important to me before everything became too much.

I suddenly stopped caring about my work. Nothing could get me re-engaged in my old career.

I had the energy to live. I wanted to be happy. So, I did whatever made me happy.

Nature was calling me. So, I began to go on several short walks a day. I noticed everything. I could smell the flowers, the lake, and the sunshine. The tiniest details leaped out at me.

My spirit guides, mother and sister, kept me company. They had been telling me for years that I needed to wake up and help raise the level of consciousness on the planet.

I began to giggle again.

Birds, bees, butterflies, and dragonflies would visit me on every walk. I could hear the trees and animals for the first time in years. I had always been able to see energy, but now I could see energy and auras as clearly as I did as a child.

I wanted to do all the things I used to love at once. I wanted to sing, dance, paint, swim, smile, laugh, and talk.

After a few weeks of getting healthier, it was time to open memory mansion. I needed to speak about everything I had never allowed myself to share. Healing would come with no longer being ashamed of my life.

My guides told me to listen to my favorite music. Which, of course, was classic rock. So, I went on YouTube and started playing everything from Journey to AC/DC to Meatloaf and Blondie.

After a few weeks of dancing and singing at the top of my lungs, much to my best friend's amusement, the lock on memory mansion broke. It was listening to Queen and Heart on repeat that did it. I always liked to play the same songs over and over.

When I felt the doors of my mansion crack open, I went to the porch and got comfortable in my favorite old chair.

That is when my eyes began to move in a rectangle, left, up, right, and down; this went on for hours, then days.

I realized I was unlocking all the memories I had stored away.

In my mind's eye, I could see myself racing through the rooms of memory mansion, ripping the boxes and shelves from the walls.

I saved the most significant room for last. I always called it the library. This is where I stored most of the 80s. When I finished, I felt like an overgrown child sitting in the middle of a thousand damaged boxes.

At some point, Gerard had come outside. He was happy but concerned about the change in my behavior. I was about to make his head pop off.

As I unfurled my memories, I opened my mouth and shared long-held secrets. After a few days of listening to me on the porch, Gerard became very concerned. I must credit him for how well he took what I shared. He only asked a few questions during my verbal exorcism.

At one point, he worried about my mental health but could see me getting stronger by the day. He had never heard me talk like that, which scared him.

About halfway through my memory boxes, I began to get very angry.

I was angry about the injustice of so much of what happened. I was mad at myself for living smaller than I should have out of embarrassment for my mistakes. I was angry that my family was gone. I was pissed at myself for how I handled much of what happened.

I had always dreamed of crucifying Jimmy and telling everyone what kind of person he was. In my dreams, I would see a dragon swooping down on Memphis to burn the places that had brought pain to my family. I even went on social media and wrote a post telling everyone I was back to scorch the Earth. Haha, I was pissed.

Outside of one sneak visit to see Shirley and Jimmy's creepy house, I shook the whole time; I had been too frightened to look them up. I was angry enough to do it finally.

That is how I found out he passed away while I was coming back to life. That made me angrier. How dare he not answer his deeds or be able to answer my questions!

Thankfully, I could never stay angry for long. I have always been far too rational for seething anger.

My favorite quote that Sister Anne Elizabeth taught me is that resentment is like drinking poison and expecting another person to die. I wanted to live. So, I forgave him and anyone who brought pain into my life.

I wanted to taste the world in a way I never had before. I wanted to be at peace and bliss.

The Age of Aquarius was approaching, and I needed to prepare.

# Chapter 65

## Age 51, South Florida

My spirit guides were very vocal about my healing journey. They were so delighted that I had finally decided to step up; they would leave nothing to chance. They had me hoovering up metaphysical reminders and listening to Solfeggio frequencies for weeks around the clock. Sound healing is so powerful!

After enjoying that one night's rest, I no longer needed to sleep. I was wide awake. I had lived like the walking dead for a decade, so I didn't need the sleep anyway.

I felt and acted like a teenager. I looked much younger than I had in years, and my hair returned to its natural color.

I added spiritual practices back to my life. In addition to drinking water and eating sustainably, I started to meditate, pray, write, go to the gym, and do yoga. That began to usher in mind, body, and soul harmony.

I began revisiting my life choices with new eyes. I was getting a do-over of all the decisions I had ever made. I decided that I was going to be a Renaissance woman.

What did I enjoy? What kind of music did I like? How did I want to dress, do my hair, and wear my makeup? What did I want to be when I grew up? Most importantly, how would I help people now that I didn't feel the need to do it secretly?

How would I bring the most authentic version of myself to the party? What name would I use? Did I even care about a name that meant nothing to me? I have not been called Cynthia "Cindy" Elliott since I was young.

My eyes had finally stopped moving in a rectangle. After a few months, I opened the last of my memories. I was no longer experiencing rage. I was excited about the future.

I had lost the depression-related weight and most of the shame I had carried throughout my life. The shame had kept me mute.

Once all of my memories were on the table, I could not help but see the unhealthy patterns that kept repeating in my life and lineage. I had always seen patterns in my work and interactions with others but never studied them in my family history.

Now, they were screaming to be addressed. I started to see that I had been reacting to life for decades. If I wasn't trying to manage tomorrow, I was analyzing yesterday to try and control or predict tomorrow.

Sure, I could manifest great things; I had even created specialties in my industry that are now studied in schools worldwide. However, all of that work was outside of me. It was about belief in something external.

Running all those years was me reacting to life. It was a fear-driven existence at the bottom of the human consciousness scale.

I would go so far as to say these ancestral cycles were killing my family far too young. I have been on the edge of chronic illness for years, something that killed many of my immediate family.

We could not be content because we kept passing unhealthy patterns down the line. Now that I was healthy, I wanted to break the chain.

The ideals of the nuclear family and the American Dream didn't help. It prevented us from seeing that attaining something, like a home or respect at work, would fix our lack of emotional intelligence and self-love.

## SHAMAN ISIS

We saw ourselves as victims without voices. Sure, society reinforced that, but we were warriors without the reward. The reward only comes when you proactively create your reality through mindful practices. Something I learned the hard way.

Over the years, I accumulated a lot of knowledge. Now, I am driven to enhance that experience with science.

# Chapter 66

## AGE 52, SOUTH FLORIDA

I immersed myself in mindful or spiritual science. Mindfulness is technically a practice within spirituality. People prefer the word mindful because they associate spirituality with religion.

Spirituality is as old as man; religion is not. Either way, mindful or spiritual practices were the answer to learning how to love myself and my life.

The coronavirus closure allowed me to change my life and rapidly expand my beliefs about the human experience.

Opening my memories brought the patterns of my past to life like a trail map. I could see the habits and cycles that trapped me and my family in mental misery.

I began understanding the power of our thoughts, beliefs, emotions, and consciousness in shaping our life experiences.

Thought habits are at the core of human pleasure and pain.

Our family and childhood experiences teach these thought habits. We only know what we grow up seeing and learning.

We are like saplings planted in a pot of soil. That soil comprises our ancestors' habits and our environment, with a dash of personal experience.

I thought I had created my way of living. It took seeing the trail of family patterns to accept that even someone who spent little time around their family repeats ancestral patterns. This happens in families until some outlier, usually a black sheep, breaks the "curse."

Think of yourself as a vintage wine. You are the essence of the time, place, and soil you were raised absorbing. You can no more escape repeating what you know than changing the bouquet of your vintage.

I realized that our thought habits dictate our mental state, our mental state dictates our emotional state, and our emotional state drives the frequency and vibration in our energy field. I call this cycle the Reality Wheel.

That vibration (vibe, feelings, mood, etc.) affects our current life experience. To change my life experience and raise my level of consciousness, I had to exchange unhealthy thought habits for high-quality thought habits.

I began to use every trigger to practice better thought habits. This is why avoiding triggers can be unhelpful. How do we see what needs work if we don't know the pattern of what causes us to react?

We all have an invisible energy field around us that acts like a beacon, calling on the universe to bring us what we are resonating with. This process places our thought habits at the core of our reality. We get sent experiences that mirror our repeating thought habits.

We decide, through what we choose to think, if the abundance we are drawing in is negative or positive. Of course, bad things happen to good people, but many more bad things happen to people struggling with unhealthy thought habits. You become a crap magnet with bad energy.

It is also challenging to manifest when you are in negative energy.

The truth is anyone can transform their life when they decide to take control of their conscious and subconscious beliefs, thoughts, and patterns. If you can get in a bad mood with stinking thinking, you can put yourself in a beautiful state with mindful living.

The fact is, we select our thoughts the same way we choose our food. It simply takes the decision to change and the commitment to practicing better thought habits for them to become your new natural.

This is the process I went through. It took months of practice, getting triggered, and more practice. Eventually, healthy thoughts became my preferred choice. Sure, like any human being, I have my moments. These days, they are few and far between.

We are so much more powerful than we have been taught to believe. We become unstoppable when we decide to unlock our full potential and live a blissful life.

Blissful living is a choice. A healthy perception of your life circumstances is a choice. This is especially important when you are dealing with tough circumstances.

We are designed to enjoy life. You read that right! Subconsciously, I decided that enjoying life wasn't an option. I was simply existing.

Changing my thought habits was the single most significant decision I ever made. It allowed me to learn to love life again.

That is where you start - with the decision to change your life experience. You decide to practice choosing healthy thought habits. You become the master of your reality by changing your perception of life.

# Chapter 67

## AGE 53, NYC

As I dug further into spiritual science, I fell in love with the work of Dr. Joe Dispenza, Greg Braden, Sadhguru, Dr. Bruce Lipton, and many of the old masters. The following are some of my takeaways from this research.

Our connection with nature has been severed with modern living, promoting a fear-driven existence. This places most people at the bottom of the consciousness scale. That is where all of the negative emotions reside. Those emotions include guilt, shame, anger, and desire.

This fear-driven existence is why mental health has become such a crisis. Media and capitalism are feasting on humanity in the lower registers of consciousness. Fear and sickness profit many big corporations. There is no financial incentive for them to support humanity in achieving higher levels of consciousness.

The corruption of our natural state is causing global misery. We must raise human consciousness as the answer to the mental health crisis. That shift in consciousness will happen if we teach everyone mindfulness practices.

Mindful practices allow people to have emotional and mental mastery. That is why I teach an emotional and mental fitness workout. We need a mental workout the same way we need a physical workout.

The mind and body are interconnected. Our thoughts and emotions influence our physical health and well-being.

I believe that our thoughts can make us sick and that many chronic illnesses are caused by a combination of negativity and greed-driven solutions to the human condition, such as genetically modified food. I have watched people worry themselves sick many times.

Chronic illness, which killed many in my family, has risen in direct correlation with capitalism. That is why we must be careful about eating anything mass-produced.

Our food is poisoning our bodies, while the media is poisoning our minds. This is why we have experienced a massive increase in chronic illness and mental health issues in recent decades. Greed has had a field day on the collective of humanity.

There is an interconnectedness to the entire universe. Ironically, quantum physics eventually agreed with ancient wisdom on the interconnectedness of all things.

The field of quantum physics has the exact definition as spirit does in spirituality. Quantum physics represents invisible moving forces that influence the physical world. Spirit in spirituality means invisible driving forces that influence the physical world. Science and spirituality have a lot in common. Science inches closer to supporting spiritual concepts every day.

We are all connected through "invisible" energy, meaning we affect each other. Imagine humanity is similar to the millions of cells in one human body. We all similarly affect each other as those cells work to make us healthy or sick. When more people live in the more enlightened levels of consciousness, such as joy and bliss, the whole of humanity gets healthier. Which is why raising human consciousness is such a game changer.

In physics, all possibilities exist in your present experience. I was always living with one foot in the past and one foot in the future. Most of us do this. It stems from the illusion that we control the outcome of things by using our history to predict the future. In retrospect, this was the single most significant waste of my life.

We are often not present in the only time we have, that moment we are currently experiencing. When we are not present, our energy loses its power and shrinks. We become dense in more ways than one. So, I had to train myself not to try and manipulate life.

When we lead with love, from a state of grace and gratitude, we expand our energy and open our experience to the most beautiful outcome in any possible moment. It may not be the outcome we were hoping for, but it is very often the outcome we need.

When we are resonating at peak potential, we become superheroes. We become masters of our energy. That is the core of this message. Become a master of your energy, and you become unstoppable.

Changing conscious and unconscious thought habits, drinking water, eating right, meditating, yoga, breathing, journaling, grounding in nature, and healing our history is the secret recipe to living in emotional, mental, physical, and spiritual harmony.

Mindful living set me free and brought peace and bliss.

These practices allowed me to heal, break the cycles, learn self-love, and become conscious.

I remember the day I realized how profoundly I had changed. For months, birds had kept me company on walks. Delicate great herons decorated my visits with nature. I took so many beautiful photos. The birds always stayed just out of reach of a good close-up.

One day, I was taking pictures when a blue heron approached me. I was so surprised that I sat down next to the bird. This experience was a meaningful sign from the universe.

Suddenly, I realized that I had stepped fully into higher consciousness. My frequency had returned to that of nature, like a child. They saw my energy signature as the same as theirs and felt at home, as did I.

I cried. I had not felt this level of joy and alignment since childhood.

Suddenly, I fully understood my mission to help raise the level of consciousness on the planet. Consciousness through mindfulness would help turn the tide of the mental health crisis and chronic illness.

My guides gave me direction for the future. I was to teach others what I had learned. I had always known this was where my life was leading. I was just afraid to be myself.

I needed to help people heal and learn the mind, body, and soul practices that create emotional mastery.

So, I wrote down the entire process. I paid particular attention to how I healed, broke the family curses, changed my thought habits, and created emotional mastery. I would teach others how to create a life and reality they love. That process grew to nine steps and three modules that teach someone to live blissfully through science. I appropriately named it Engineering Joy.

Finally, my guides shared that we needed to grow human consciousness to be better prepared to handle what the age of Aquarius and AI would bring to Earth.

We must use the mental health crisis to teach as many people as possible how to develop life mastery.

By making mental fitness as appreciated and supported as physical health, we can turn a crisis into the single most significant opportunity for humanity.

AI will usher in abundance unlike we have ever seen. However, human consciousness will decide what that abundance will be like for all humanity. It is a priceless opportunity to build a better way of living that benefits society and the planet.

The more people we have living with healthy thought habits and higher levels of consciousness, the more blissful the entire global collective will feel.